RURAL POVERTY, EMPOWERMENT AND SUSTAINABLE LIVELIHOODS

Rural Poverty, Empowerment and Sustainable Livelihoods

Edited by
JOSEPH MULLEN
Institute for Development Policy and Management
University of Manchester

Routledge
Taylor & Francis Group

LONDON AND NEW YORK

First published 1999 by Ashgate Publishing

Reissued 2018 by Routledge
2 Park Square, Milton Park, Abingdon, Oxon, OX14 4RN
711 Third Avenue, New York, NY 10017, USA

Routledge is an imprint of the Taylor & Francis Group, an informa business

Publisher's Note
The publisher has gone to great lengths to ensure the quality of this reprint but points out that some imperfections in the original copies may be apparent.

Disclaimer
The publisher has made every effort to trace copyright holders and welcomes correspondence from those they have been unable to contact.

A Library of Congress record exists under LC control number: 99063208

ISBN 13: 978-1-138-35245-2 (hbk)
ISBN 13: 978-0-429-43476-1 (ebk)

Contents

Acknowledgements

Permission was granted by the Commonwealth Secretariat to reproduce the two papers given by Kweku Appiah and Fadil Abbas at the Regional Workshop on Poverty Reduction Strategies and Programmes and is gratefully acknowledged. The Workshop, which was held in November 1996 at Arusha, Tanzania, was sponsored by the Commonwealth Secretariat, welcomed delegates from the five East African countries of Tanzania, Uganda, Kenya, Mozambique and Malawi to discuss regional strategies for poverty reduction. The Case Studies of Ghana and Malaysia were presented as comparative experiences for analysis. The cooperation of Messrs. Dick Gold and Brian Kerr of the EIDD Division of the Secretariat is much appreciated.

The editor wishes to thank the team of authors for sharing their knowledge and insights with the community of academics and practitioners from Asia, Africa and Latin America who are the core participants of the Rural Poverty Alleviation Programme and the DSA Study Group on Rural Development. Particular thanks is due to Mrs Cerries Smith (1938-1998) who was responsible for the organisation and administration of the Symposium and typing the first draft of the papers. She also served as Course Administrator to the Rural Poverty Alleviation Programme at IDPM since its inception in 1992 and contributed substantially to its success. She will be sadly missed by the many she endeared herself to at IDPM. Cerries has prematurely departed from this life and this book is dedicated to her memory. The work could never have been completed without the constant encouragement of my wife Patricia to whom I am deeply grateful. Karen Hunt conscientiously typed the final drafts for the publishers despite numerous interruptions and my endemic procrastination. The patience of the editors at Ashgate and their endurance when several deadlines were passed, has been remarkable.

Joseph Mullen
Institute for Development Policy
and Management
University of Manchester
Fax: 0161 273 8829
e-mail: Joseph.Mullen@man.ac.uk

List of Contributors

Fadil Azim Abbas is Director of the Redistribution Section, Economic Planning Unit, Prime Minister's Department, Government of Malaysia, Kuala Lumpur.

Salehuddin Ahmed is Director of the Bureau of NGO Affairs, Office of the Prime Minister, Government of Bangladesh. Former Director of the Bangladesh Academy for Rural Development, Comilla.

Kweku O A Appiah is Director of the Social Development Division, National Development Planning Commission, Accra, Government of Ghana. He is also coordinator of the African Poverty Network.

Liu Fengqin is Director of International Relations, Technological University of Beijing, China.

Anthony Hall is Senior Lecturer in Social Planning in Developing Countries at the London School of Economics and Political Science.

Wolfgang Herbinger, Bruce Crawshaw and John Shaw at time of writing were staff members of the United Nations World Food Programme, Rome.

Joseph Mullen is Director of the Rural Poverty Alleviation Programme at the Institute for Development Policy and Management, University of Manchester; Convenor of the Rural Development Study Group of the Development Studies Association of the UK and Ireland. Former staff member of the International Fund for Agricultural Development of the United Nations.

Jane Oliver is a Research Fellow at the School for Development Studies, University of East Anglia.

Introduction

Joseph Mullen

The elimination of absolute poverty has become the overriding objective of many inter-national development agencies, national governments and non-governmental organisations. Multilateral financial institutions such as the World Bank and the International Fund for Agricultural Development (IFAD) view poverty reduction as a central tenet of their organisational mandate. Similarly, major bilateral aid agencies including those of Australia, Canada, Finland, Ireland, Netherlands, Sweden and the United Kingdom, in the wake of the World Social Summit held at Copenhagen in 1995, are committed to poverty elimination as a key criterion of both bilateral country partnerships and of programme support.

However, poverty elimination or alleviation is not exclusively an exogenous, donor driven phenomenon. The majority of country governments have also committed themselves to the same Programme of Action of the World Social Summit and many have since 1995, pursued substantive poverty reduction initiatives in terms of policies, realignment of public expenditures to address deprivation and investment in the productive capacities of low income populations. Vibrant civil society associations, representing the poor themselves or working among the poor, have undertaken practical micro-level initiatives, to protect vulnerable livelihoods.

Ultimately, the most resilient and sustainable poverty reduction initiatives are strongly dependent upon the level of commitment, determination and organisational capacity of the poor themselves. The ability of the state to intervene in key areas of social protection, and implement policies to enhance the enabling micro-economic environment in which the poor live, has been substantially reduced. External and domestic constraints relating to indebtedness, weak institutional capacity, and inadequate accountability have all contributed to eroding the ability of the state to intervene. Political factors which threaten the destabilisation of the state itself such as border conflicts, civil wars and ethnic cleansing exacerbate poverty and have led to the collapse of institutional provision of health, education and markets. Increased military expenditure to ensure internal and external security further weakens the capacity of the state to address poverty and social issues.

Poverty reduction efforts are increasingly being implemented in hostile environments, against backgrounds of human rights violations, indebtedness, corruption, oppression of minorities and structured discrimination against the poor, designed to induce powerlessness and passivity. The lessons of successful initiatives to alleviate poverty and address its causes suggests the need for strong local institutions grounded in local realities which can be supported by like-minded partner agencies at national or international levels. The key activities in this respect are enabling policy frameworks, capacity strengthening, supporting local initiatives and developing human resources, which are a central theme of this book. A second theme refers to sustainable livelihoods or the acknowledgement of the integrated nature of poverty reduction which encompasses resource accessibility and management, control over assets, markets, household incomes, health, education, gender sensitivity, social inclusion and environmental preservation.

This book sets out to explore the nature of poverty and interpret it across a range of policy reforms and project interventions in different geographical settings. It is the culmination of a team effort involving development academics and professionals from diverse national and disciplinary backgrounds who came together in two distinct fora. The first event was held at the University of Manchester's Institute for Development Policy and Management, whose Rural Poverty Alleviation Programme hosted the Development Study Association's Rural Development Study Group Symposium on the theme of the book's title. It took place in November 1995. The second major input to the book are two papers from the Commonwealth Secretariat's Regional Workshop for East and Central Africa on Strategies for Poverty Reduction to which the editor was a principal resource person. Permission to reproduce these papers by the Commonwealth Secretariat is gratefully acknowledged.

Underpinning the rational and logically argued approach of the different authors is the conviction that in humanitarian terms, it is morally and ethically repugnant that over 1.3 billion people are currently living in conditions of endemic hunger and poverty while the wealth of a minority continues to increase exponentially. There is a wide ranging analysis by different authors of some of the causes leading to this situation: these would include the inequitable distribution of wealth, lack of access to productive resources, ethnic conflict, insufficient participation by the poor in the decisions which affect their lives and the deleterious impact of policy reforms upon survival and coping strategies of the poor. However poverty alleviation initiatives include a wide range of individual and civil society activities supported by representative community-based organisations, which affirm the poor as active agents of their endogenous development over generations. It is upon this tradition of survival at the family and community level that form the basis upon which inter-generational transfers of poverty can be halted.

Participation in the context of the field management of food-aided projects in Ethiopia is described in Chapter 1 by three staff members of the World Food Programme (WFP); Herbinger, Crawshaw and Shaw. Participation, it is argued, is significant in bringing about a people-centred approach to achieving equitable and sustainable growth. These assumptions are tested in the context of a WFP land and infrastructure rehabilitation project in Ethiopia and lessons of experience, arising from constraints and opportunities are grounded in the realities of a complex and highly instructive case study.

In Chapter 2, Anthony Hall approaches the theme of livelihood sustainability and empowerment within the context of productive conservation in Brazilian Amazonia. Echoing the theme of statelessness developed by Mullen in the following chapter, Hall argues that, in the absence of effective state action from the centre to protect the environment, the initiative for environmental action to protect rural livelihoods has fallen to socio-environmental groups to protect the natural resources base upon which their livelihood depends; while simultaneously developing compatible productive activities which support the livelihoods.

The essay by Mullen on Statelessness, Ethnicity and Conflict is situated within the context of reconstruction of village communities in Somalia and develops further the themes of village-based rural development and local level participation by Ahmed and Herbinger et alia. Chapter 3, gives an account of the impact of civil war on village level institutions and on rural productivity, with particular emphasis on the role of ethnicity and local reconciliation initiatives, based upon the restoration of traditional forms of governance as a new form of empowerment and livelihood sustainability. The conflicting military and humanitarian mandates of United Nations peace keeping troops in a complex emergency situation is analysed with a view to reconciling external intervention with endogenous conflict resolution and institutions of traditional governance.

Transition and change are recurring themes in Liu Fengqin's chapter on rural poverty alleviation in China. She outlines the key role of agriculture in poverty reduction policy, the emphasis on market-led reforms based substantially on production-enhancing measures rather than relief measures.

In Chapter 5, a seminal paper by Dr Salehuddin Ahmed outlines the mould-breaking initiatives in rural development initiated at Comilla in Bangladesh and illustrates how village-based, people-driven rural development systems have evolved into systems of empowerment and sustainable livelihoods.

In Chapters 6 and 7 two country case studies are presented focusing on national policy frameworks relating to poverty reduction. Kweku Appiah in Chapter 6 argues that poverty reduction and rural development are virtually synonymous in Ghana, in view of the high percentage of the population dependent upon rural production systems for their livelihood and well being. The vulnerability of a fragile economy to externally generated shocks and donor-driven reforms was reflected in the substantial deterioration of quality of life indicators which, in turn, generated interventions to mitigate the negative social side effects. The lessons to be drawn from the Ghanaian experience are eloquently described in the concluding section. The experience of a rapidly growing Asian economy, highlights factors which are also shared in a number of respects, with low income nations in Africa and Latin America. The proactive role of the state in promoting ethnic harmony, redistribution of wealth and opportunity as preconditions to the pursuit of poverty-reducing growth challenges the received wisdom on the receding state. The policy initiatives were locally driven and included an emphasis on social and spiritual values within the context of a culture of merit and excellence. Poverty alleviation efforts were sharply focused on hard core poverty, but the intractability of reducing poverty levels to single digits is broadly recognised. The concluding section of this paper by Dr Fadil Azim Abbas outlines interesting lessons to be drawn from the Malaysian experience.

The concluding chapter by Oliver examines the legitimacy of claims of NGOs to being at the forefront of micro level participatory development, primarily by challenging the consistency between internal organisational behavioural patterns and the participative philosophy of field operations. The issue of institutional transparency emerges as a critical validating assumption underpinning the legitimacy of NGO intervention in poverty alleviation.

1 Beneficiary Participation in Context: Practical Experiences from a Food-aided Project in Ethiopia

WOLFGANG HERBINGER, BRUCE CRAWSHAW
AND JOHN SHAW

Abstract

Beneficiary participation should not be seen as a panacea for overcoming all problems of development. It can play a strategic role, however, in bringing about a people-centred approach to achieving equitable and sustainable growth for which, in the real world, trade-offs and compromises will be necessary. In a major World Food Programme-assisted land and infrastructure rehabilitation project in Ethiopia, a beneficiary participation approach has been introduce in an attempt to improve the appropriateness and sustainability of project activities. Based on this experience, the paper examines some of the constraints to incorporating beneficiary participation in the design and implementation of development projects. These include: increased planning costs, which may or may not be balanced by improved prospects for the sustainability of the assets created; conflict between local community priorities and the objectives of governments and aid agencies; private versus public and community benefits; raising the expectations of communities compared to the ability of development authorities to deliver; and local knowledge versus technical expertise. Beneficiary participation has the potential to be an effective instrument, but if it is to be realized, attention must be paid to its limitations and constraints.

1

Introduction

This paper examines some of the conflicts and compromises involved in adopting beneficiary participation as part of the process of designing and implementing externally-assisted development projects. It draws on the experience of the World Food Programme (WFP) in a major land and infrastructure rehabilitation project in Ethiopia to illustrate some of the practical implications of beneficiary participation in the real world of development assistance.

Participatory development: a critique

Renewed interest has been expressed in beneficiary participation in the design, implementation and evaluation of development projects and in the concept of 'participatory development'. One of the most comprehensive recent treatments of the subject (Oakley, 1991), drawing on wide-ranging literature on the subject as well as material in the project files of a number of United Nations agencies and several non-governmental organizations (NGOs), makes four overriding points:

- First, the rhetoric concerning people's participation still far outweighs the practice.

- Second, 'participation' defies any single attempt at definition or interpretation, and means different things to different people.

- Third, there is no one model or single way of implementing people's participation, but there are now a number of experiences that could help practitioners confronting similar situations (the publication contains a number of case studies).

- Fourth, to be undertaken thoroughly and well, people's participation requires policy commitment and professional understanding: it is not a soft option for solving the problems of governments and aid agencies.

WFP's overall experience echoes these basic conclusions in introducing beneficiary participation into the design and implementation of the development projects it supports with food aid.

The World Food Programme perspective

WFP has over 30 years of experience in working with communities, using food aid to support development projects to help increase the self-reliance of poor and hungry people. There are three main factors in WFP-assisted development projects: (a) members of the local communities who participate in the project, the main primary beneficiaries from the development assets created; (b) national government agencies, which implement the projects; and (c) WFP, which provides most of the external resources.

From the WFP perspective, the introduction of beneficiary participation is based on the belief that sustainable development can only be achieved if project beneficiaries have a personal or collective stake in the development activities undertaken. Projects are more likely to 'succeed' - their activities and benefits are likely to continue to be realized beyond the provision of external assistance - to the extent that the kinds and pace of changes introduced with food assistance make sound economic sense and are socially feasible from the perspective of the beneficiaries. Such issues as land use patterns, including tenure arrangements; access to productive resources and services; and availability and allocation of household labour are of particular concern.

A WFP-assisted land and infrastructure rehabilitation project in Ethiopia, which directly, benefits hundreds of thousands of people a year in some of the most food-insecure regions of the country, illustrates one approach adopted by WFP towards beneficiary participation, and highlights some of the practical implications.

The Ethiopia example

WFP has been assisting rural rehabilitation activities in Ethiopia for more than 20 years. Until recently, the basic approach had changed little over the years. Until recently, the basic approach had changed little over the. Food aid has been provided to small-scale farmers as an incentive for them to undertake soil and water conservation activities in food-deficit areas. There is general agreement that massive and widespread soil erosion, mainly caused by water run-off, is a major reason for the low level of food production of most small-scale farmers in the highlands of Ethiopia. By arresting soil erosion and through measures that improve agricultural productivity, it is expected that food production, and hence food security, will increase, and the need for food aid will decline, thereby enabling WFP to phase out its assistance.

The initial phase of the project began in the early 1970s, largely as a part of a relief assistance programme which aimed also at achieving some developmental effects. The project quickly operated on a massive scale, involving hundreds of thousands of workers throughout the country. During this early period, all planning was done by the central government, with development targets or quotas (numbers of kilometres of bunds to be constructed; numbers of trees to be planted, etc.) given to regional authorities, who in turn passed them on to local government authorities at the awraja (district) level and from there to the technical experts/development agents assigned to each peasant association (PA - local farming communities). PA officials were responsible for mobilizing farmers to carry out the work.

A considerable amount of work was achieved, mainly as a result of mass labour campaigns. Standard work norms and erosion control measures were uniformly applied throughout the project areas, irrespective of local conditions. Equity was not considered an issue as all works were carried out on 'community' land. Farmers had little opportunity to express their concerns, or to undertake activities that were of greater interest to them. As a result, they often had little stake in the structures that were built; and they could not voice their opinions concerning the work executed (for example, on how to design and space soil bunds so that they might take up less land or allow more turning space for the oxen that pulled the plough). Farmers were simply told what to do, and what food rations they would receive in return.

The result of this centralized, top-down approach was that, in some cases, farmers were mainly interested in receiving WFP food rations; they had little interest in the actual activities they were paid to undertake, or in the long-term benefits that were expected to be achieved as a result of the works completed. In a few cases (i.e. in locations where the works were technically inappropriate and resulted in decreasing production levels instead of contributing to an increase), the same area was repeatedly worked on for several years, as this was a convenient way to, at least, earn food wages. The Government-appointed technicians responsible for implementing the project tended to select those areas and activities that produced achievements in the shortest time and with the least effort, thus enabling them to fulfil their work quotas as quickly as possible. In the circumstances, it was not surprising that the quality of work was sometimes poor and that occasionally the structures built collapsed, or were deliberately sabotaged. Despite increasing pressure from WFP and a technical support project assisted by the United Nations Food and Agriculture Organization (FAO), the previous Ethiopian administration was unwilling to change this top-down, centralist approach.

In the late 1980s, with the weakening of the central planning system, and later the change of Government, attempts were made by the concerned Government ministries to introduce a more 'user-friendly' planning and implementation system. This initiative culminated in an approach called 'minimum planning', in which more emphasis was placed on devolving responsibility for designing and implementing projects to the local level. During 1990, more than 1,000 Government technicians and development agents were trained in the application of this approach, which was based on involving local people in prioritizing their communities' development problems, helping to identify appropriate development activities (these had previously been mainly focused on soil and water conservation) and preparing community sketch maps to assist in planning and locating sites for these activities.

The 'minimum planning' approach was developed with FAO technical support. However, as the previous Ethiopian government was reluctant to give up on its centralist approach to planning and administration, the actual implementation of the 'minimum planning' approach was suspended and the FAO project came to an end in 1991.

Local Level Participatory Planning (LLPP)

Faced with increasing poor project performance, WFP revived the idea of making project planning more community-oriented and participatory, based on the experience of the 'minimum planning' approach. 'Local Level Participatory Planning' (LLPP) was thus introduced into the WFP-assisted project.

LLPP's primary objective is to involve people in the entire development process, from project identification to completion, and thus focus project activities on their priorities. A major challenge for the LLPP approach is to balance short-term and longer-run benefits, as the project basically functions as an employment-based safety net, i.e. providing work and food rations needed in the short-term and, at the same time, creating developmental assets that will help local communities become more self-reliant in the longer-term. The project builds on the concept of farming systems and recognition of the need to integrate water development, rural infrastructure construction and soil conservation together with agronomic measures - agroforestry, silvipasture and livestock production. Another objective of LLPP is to sensitize participating communities to take into account the special needs of the poorest households in the identification and design of food-for-work activities, including those that best meet their needs.

In 1992, LLPP was introduced in eight selected pilot areas. In conjunction, a study was undertaken on how to strengthen socio-economic considerations in participatory project planning.

Experience from the pilot areas has been highly encouraging. Therefore, the next step has been to undertake large scale training of Government technicians and development agents so that they are able to replicate the approach throughout the WFP project area. Some 900 Government technicians had been trained in the LLPP approach by early 1994. At the same time, the LLPP approach has been adopted in areas not covered by the WFP-assisted project.

The step-by-step approach of LLPP is as follows:

(a) the local Government development agent calls a general assembly of the community;

(b) he/she explains the LLPP approach;

(c) a planning team of five to eight male and female community members is elected by the assembly;

(d) with the help of the planning team the development agent carries out an initial socio-economic survey;

(e) the project area is determined, usually ranging between 300 and 800 hectares;

(f) two site maps are drawn up - a base map, and a development map on which the activities to be undertaken is located; and

(g) agreement for each project site is reached on the activities to be undertaken, their timing, the expected outputs and required inputs.

6

Figure 1.1

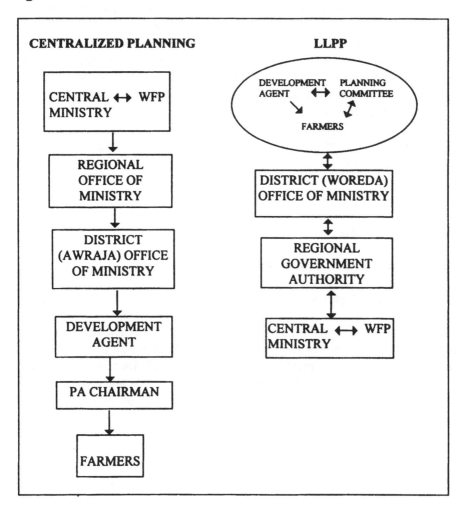

The first step in the implementation of the LLPP approach involves holding meetings with local communities to explain the concept of participatory planning, emphasizing that community members themselves will decide which activities to undertake. Simple land-use and land classification maps are drawn up by the technicians with the help of community members. The next step in the process is a 'problem identification exercise' in which the community draws up and ranks a list of problems it faces - for example, water shortage, land erosion, access to markets, etc. Other steps that follow include: identifying particular target groups in the community who should receive assistance; and analyzing the local socio-economic constraints to development, including those specific to women. The steps are carried out with the full participation of members of the community. The end result is an agreed 'community development plan' specifying the activities to be carried out, inputs needed, work plans and priorities. The plan and a development map serve as the basis not only for undertaking the work, but also for tracking progress.

Adaption of LLPP procedures to the socio-economic, cultural and administrative conditions of each locality is of crucial importance. Development agents are encouraged to flexibly apply the LLPP approach as long as they keep with its basic principles and objectives.

Problems with LLPP

Several problems have been encountered in implementing LLPP.

Costs of the LLPP approach

LLPP (and, by extension, all participatory planning) is particularly intensive in terms of staff resources and time required, at least during its initial stages. It takes time to organize meetings with farmers, talk to them and, after years of top-down planning, win their trust. A process of trial and error, in which community members may revise ad rework earlier decisions in the light of experience, is inevitable, and even desirable. In the eight pilot sites in which LLPP has been introduced, it took up to two months to prepare the plans. Given that these pilot sites were selected near transport routes and Government centres, and received priority consideration in terms of technical assistance, inputs and backstopping, the 'norm' would be expected to be even longer. Once the plans are completed, their implementation requires follow-up and backstopping by local Government technical staff, including possible further revisions.

The pay-off is expected to come from greater efficiency in the use of development resources and in terms of achieving more sustainable, lasting benefits for the community. So far, there is little empirical data to confirm that participatory approaches do result in more sustainable results. On the other hand, there is evidence to support that failure to involve local communities in the decision-making process results in activities that are contrary to the interests of target communities, and thus result in wasted aid

8

resources. There are also initial reports that time requirements tend to fall the more experience has been gained with the LLPP approach ad the wider it is accepted.

Conflict of objectives

The major internal conflict of the LLPP approach is that the different actors (local community, Government, WFP) have different objectives and expectations. This reflects the basic dichotomy inherent in beneficiary participation:

- participation ensures that project designers and managers have more complete information available to them to undertake their work;

- participation means people can take control of their own lives, and do not need professional designers or managers, i.e. that it 'deprofessionalizes' development and empowers local communities.

Like most development agencies, WFP tries to steer a middle course between these two views. This is rarely possible in practice. A prime objective for *WFP* is to improve the targeting of food aid to food-insecure households in food-deficit areas and, with the help of LLPP, to achieve more sustainable results.

The *Government* has two main objectives. For those institutions concerned with meeting food relief requirements, the prime objective is to ensure that food aid reaches the target beneficiaries, and that it does not disrupt local farm activities and food production. For the development ministries, the important goal is to achieve sustainable rural development by arresting environmental degradation and improving agricultural productivity.

For neither the Government nor for WFP has empowerment of the local community been a primary objective of LLPP. Rather, the main motive has been to improve the management of the implementation of project activities and to try to achieve a more sustained impact from the project.

The *local communities* see LLPP as at least a beginning to their empowerment - increasing their ability to take control of their own affairs. Elements of the LLPP which encourage empowerment, include: the establishment of a planning committee that is elected by the community; initiation of a review process of problems and issues faced by the community; the joint assessment of the problems; deciding on project activities to be undertaken; having a local planning committee taking responsibility for implementation and monitoring; improving the capacity of

9

the community to analyze their own situation and act collectively on it. Awareness is also created of the particular needs of the poor and hungry, and ways are analyzed on how best to assist them through the project. Thus, LLPP does seem to have initiated a process of local empowerment - an unforeseen effect of the need to improve project implementation and accountability. However, as Midgley (1986) has pointed out, true decentralization and empowerment can only be expected to occur where local bodies have control over financial resources.

Increased empowerment, even in the limited manner attained at the WFP-assisted project sites, can result in increased tensions within the community. Food aid has obvious short-term benefits for participants. The local community might therefore be expected to try to obtain as much food aid as they can get. In the food-deficit areas of Ethiopia, food rations are a particularly valuable and a sought-after addition to household resources. Consequently, decisions on who in the community participates in project activities directly affect the interests of all members of the community. Traditional holders of power are usually well represented in the planning committees. This has implications for the choice of activities that are undertaken.

Despite these concerns, communities seem keen to take on greater decision-making responsibilities. In the sense that the concerns of the community are fundamentally different from the concerns of WFP and the Government, this may result in direct conflict among the parties concerned.

Private versus public benefits

A potential weakness of any exclusively community-based participatory approach is the level at which it operates. Project activities are targeted on selected communities with up to 800 hectares per site, i.e. on a relatively small area and at a relatively small target population. Such plans cannot readily include inter-communal 'public' works that could absorb the increasing number of landless labourers who may need food aid the most, but who do not come exclusively from one or other targeted community. As land in Ethiopia becomes increasingly allocated to individuals, it is inevitable that LLPP operates mainly on individual farmer's plots. Community works such as the construction of roads, earth dams and ponds, are limited in comparison, although some positive experiences have been made with inter-community collaboration in these areas.

As pointed out above, for the ministry responsible for the implementation of the project, achieving overall equity is less important

10

than achieving soil and water conservation objectives, mainly through the construction of terraces and bunds. These structures have most appeal to the relatively wealthier farmers, who have greater expectations of maintaining (even adding to) their land holdings. They have least attraction for the poorest farmers. Wealth, to the extent that it can be accumulated by the less well off, is more often kept in the form of livestock, particularly goats and sheep. This has severe implications for local environment protection. Much of the soil erosion results from over-stocking on mountain slopes. The issue of grazing animals on 'communal' hillsides is a vexed, and potentially explosive, problem in rural Ethiopia.

Under a participatory approach, which includes 'technical' advice from Government development agents, it is easy to see how decisions could be taken that result in channelling greater benefits to the richer community members. The LLPP approach seeks to reduce negative distributional effects by making a deliberate effort to maximise the involvement of all categories of people in the planning of activities and by building on existing traditional strategies to help the poorest members of the community.

Raised expectations

Increased participation by beneficiaries in project design and implementation does not necessarily resolve underlying structural issues. For example, in many of the listed concerns of farmers, the small size of farm plots has been frequently mentioned as being of fundamental significance for most of the food problems faced by farm families. Land tenure issues and the potentially vexed question of the ownership of grazing lands are also major problems facing Ethiopian farmers. LLPP does not resolve these issues. Indeed, by raising overall expectations, it may serve to highlight such structural problems, and so increase local conflict.

Nevertheless, the LLPP approach of discussing and recording the full list of problems facing a community is a deliberate process. Only in this way can the project obtain a sense of priorities of the activities it is able to directly support with food aid. For example, animal health problems are often mentioned as a top priority for the farmers. This is not a concern that the food-aided project itself can deal with. Problems falling within the scope of the project, such as lack of access roads or soil erosion, may only be ranked third or fourth in the list of priorities. Follow-up dialogue is therefore used to reach agreement on what activities should be implemented with food assistance.

In some cases, the project can act as a catalyst. Priority activities that can not be supported by the food-aided project have been communicated to other Government ministries and in a number of cases these have been acted upon (e.g. animal vaccination campaigns have been triggered by LLPP).

Local knowledge versus technical expertise

Local knowledge and preferences may differ from the advice of professional experts, largely because of socio-cultural differences (tradition), considerations of efficiency or different time horizons. Poor farmers in food-deficit areas in Ethiopia tend to be concerned with their immediate food supplies and incomes. Government agencies and technical experts, particularly in the field of environmental protection, tend to look to longer-term benefits.

LLPP has tried to overcome these conflicts by working first with those communities, or sections of a community, that are most open to new ideas and interested in starting new project activities. After a few months of implementation, neighbouring communities have often requested to be included in the project activities.

It has also been necessary to adopt less technically efficient compromises as part of the price of beneficiary participation. One issue that stands out in the history of the WFP-assisted project in Ethiopia is the distance maintained between the bunds and terraces built by farmers to prevent soil erosion. Technical experts have argued that a terrace and bund should be built for every vertical meter of slope in order to control soil erosion. However, in many cases, cultivated land in the highlands of Ethiopia is so steep that this directive meant that terraces were too small to allow farmers to use ox-ploughs. (There is a direct relationship in many parts of Ethiopia between the use of ox-drawn ploughs and the size of harvest achieved.) After the introduction of LLPP, compromise has been reached on this technical norm and, except for low rainfall areas, bunds and terraces are now often built on every two vertical meters of slope. The result is less effective in terms of reducing soil erosion, but more acceptable to the farmers.

Conclusions

Beneficiary participation, if it is to work, requires a high degree of delegation of authority: to the communities, to the local Government development agent, to the implementing ministry, to the WFP country office. Beneficiary participation thus implies that any blueprint project document signed at the central level has to allow for a process of trial and error by all actors. The process of achieving a compromise position might be as important as the actual decision itself. An understanding and acceptance of this more fluid approach to decision making is fundamental to the successful implementation of beneficiary participation.

In spite of the caveats described in this paper, the LLPP approach does represent a genuine attempt to bring planning closer to farmers. Implementation of the LLPP approach is a formidable task. Yet the results of the first year's experience are highly encouraging. Local communities have welcomed the opportunity to be involved in the selection and design of development activities that will benefit them directly. It remains to be seen if the impact and sustainability of these activities will thereby be enhanced. As a side effect, empowerment of local communities is occurring. However, whether this will result in improved community development, or encourage local rivalries and conflicts, is as yet unclear. Beneficiary participation is not a panacea for all the problems facing development. But it does offer the means to help overcome many of the most basic stumbling blocks - if introduced with full awareness of the problems and potential.

References

Carucci, V. et al (1994), Monitoring of the nation-wide local level participatory plan preparation in WFP project 2488 assisted region, Final Draft, WFP, Rome (mimeo).

Hogg, R. (1993), Socio-Economic considerations: appraisal mission WFP Project Ethiopia 2488/III - Rehabilitation and development of rural lands and infrastructure, WFP, Rome (mimeo).

Midgley, J. (1986), *Community Participation, Social Development and the State*, Methuen, London.

Oakley, P. et al (1991), *Projects with People: the practice of participation in rural development*, Geneva.

2 Social Movements, Empowerment and Productive Conservation: The Case of Brazilian Amazonia

ANTHONY HALL[1]

Amazonia under threat: biodiversity and sociodiversity

The most critical issue currently facing those concerned for the future of Brazilian Amazonia and its people is the question of ecological and human sustainability. That is, how to promote the sustainable or non-destructive use of a dwindling natural resource base for the purpose of supporting the livelihoods of the rural population. Development policies for Amazonia have resulted in a marked loss of biodiversity. However, the socio-economic base and cultures of Amazonia's populations have also come under increasing threat as their resource base is undermined. This affects both the Amerindian population of some 150,000 as well the much larger number of rural inhabitants and their families, about eight million native *caboclos* and more recent immigrants. Small farmers in Brazilian Amazonia have, by and large, been unable to establish stable, appropriate, sedentary farming systems but have, instead, been locked into a vicious circle of frontier occupation and ecological destruction as the result of unequal access to land, use of inappropriate farming technologies imported from other regions and a general lack of government support.

The conservation of ecosystems based wholly or partly on common property resources is one important means of helping to redress this imbalance. In many parts of Amazonia, schemes are under way which allow natural resources to be used for the economic benefit of local populations while ensuring that these resources are preserved for use by future generations, a process which this author has labelled 'productive conservation' (Hall 1997a). It is argued in this chapter that the single most

14

important force working in favour of productive conservation in Brazilian Amazonia is the phenomenon of socio-environmental movements. Increasingly in Amazonia, in the absence of effective State action from the centre to protect the environment, local groups are mobilising to take the initiative in resisting destructive pressures on the natural resources which underpin their livelihoods. Such action is beginning to form the basis for new models of ecological and social sustainability peculiar to sub-ecosystems in the region, enabling distinctive groups of farmers and extractivists to reconcile two aims which have come increasingly into direct conflict with each other in recent years as official development policies for the region have put increasing pressure on the resource base. These goals are: (a) to develop productive activities which support their livelihoods while, (b) preserving the natural capital upon which these livelihoods depend. It is argued here that socio-environmental movements have distinctive characteristics which enable them to perform this dual role. This is expressed in terms of their capacity to act in self-defence, their negotiating skills, resource management capacity and their ability to form strategic alliances with external groups. Combinations of such attributes has given local communities the ability to play an increasingly powerful and innovative role in the field of environmental management in the Brazilian Amazon region.

From 'frontier economics' to 'eco-development'

There has been at least a partial evolution in the way Amazonia's environmental problems are perceived and which solutions are deemed by national planners and policy-makers to be the most appropriate (Hall 1997b). To use the terminology adopted by Colby (1990), a shift has taken place from the crude 'frontier economics' paradigm of the 1970s towards 'environmental protectionism' and 'resource management' in the 1980s and 1990s.

A 'frontier economics' perspective views nature as offering an infinite supply of physical resources for human benefit and as a sink for pollution and environmental degradation, which human ingenuity and benevolent technological advance will somehow deal with automatically. Non-scarce resources need not, by definition, be used efficiently and there is thus no need for them to be included in economic calculations of growth. Little or no thought is given to the peoples and economies which depend on these assets and policies are not directed at serving their needs, resulting in a vicious circle of poverty and environmental destruction. This paradigm describes perfectly official Amazon settlement strategies of the 1970s based on highway construction, cattle-ranching, land speculation and guided small farmer settlement.[2]

The environmental consequences of such a development pattern have been well documented; forest loss, destruction of flora and fauna, soil erosion and leaching, fertility loss, declining biodiversity and climatic changes at local, regional and possibly global levels. Social impacts have tended to receive less attention but have been no less severe; rural violence due to conflicts among peasant farmers, Amerindian groups and large landowners over access to land, growing food insecurity and worsening social indicators (Branford and Glock 1985; Hall 1989). Domestic policy-making for Amazonia has been based on the pursuit of a range of geopolitical, commercial and political goals, leaving little room for the incorporation of ecological or social considerations.

A crude 'frontier economics' perspective has been in part been superseded in most developing countries by the 'environmental protection' paradigm. This involves legalising the environment as an economic externality and concentrating on policies aimed at damage limitation. Command-and-control regulatory mechanisms, such as environmental protection agencies and environmental impact assessments tend to become institutionalised. Small areas of common property are set aside for perpetuation in their original, pristine condition as national parks, wilderness reserves or conservation areas, increasingly linked to eco-tourism. At the global level, the World Conservation Strategy has, since the early 1980s, advocated a wide-ranging approach based on neo-Malthusian precepts. Overriding concerns are those of curtailing demand for scarce resources through population policies and identifying the carrying capacity of ecosystems. Strongly echoing a wildlife management approach, ecology is seen as setting strict limits on human actions for development in a A 'conservation or disaster' scenario (Adams 1990, p. 47).

In Brazil, conservationism has been the major approach adopted by policy-makers for environmental care. It may be traced back to the early 1970s, when the Environmental Secretariat (SEMA) was set up following the United Nations Conference on the Human Environment, held in Stockholm in 1972, and the first Federal Ecological Stations were established. These numbered 26 by 1992 and covered 3.2 million hectares (Nogueira-Neto 1992). President Sarney's nationalistic 'Nossa Natureza'

(*Our Nature*) campaign and the setting up of the Brazilian Environment Institute (IBAMA) in 1989, along with the National Environment Programme (PNMA) of 1990, have also been predicated on the same basic assumption that the key to protection lies in State-sponsored vigilance backed by sanctions. Current priorities include agro-ecological zoning to inform the planning process, the demarcation of conservation units (such as national parks and reserves) and a nation-wide system of environmental agencies to license activities such as logging, to catch offenders and impose punishments where necessary. The US$250 million 'G-7 Programme to Conserve the Brazilian Rainforest', announced at the Houston Summit in July 1990, as its title implies, is also quite preservationist in its policy prescriptions and major lines of funding, although major strides have been made in the direction of promoting productive conservation strategies from local to regional levels (Hall 1997b).

The 'environmental protection' paradigm, on its own, has serious limitations as a tool for sustaining stocks of physical resources. Firstly, parks and other protected areas can never account for more than a small proportion of national territory, leaving the remainder, by definition, 'unprotected'. Some 9 per cent of Brazilian Amazonia is officially protected in 119 'conservation units' (although the figure rises to 25 per cent if indigenous reserves are included). Secondly, the management and policing capabilities of federal and state-level environmental agencies are very limited, to the point of being farcically inadequate in an area as vast as Amazonia. Thirdly, the ecosystem is still seen as external to the economy and not as an integral part of development policy-making, so that benefits arising from environmentally sound activities are not properly recognised. Development planning under this model takes no account, for example, of the importance to environmental stability of those producers who have already developed sustainable systems of natural resource use.

Simple protectionism alone is no longer regarded as an adequate mechanism for minimising ecological destruction and promoting ecological balance. Protective practices are still common and necessary under certain circumstances but, increasingly, they coexist with the 'resource management' approach. This concept emerged in the late 1980s as a major theme in reports such as those of the Brundtland Commission (1987). Highlighting the economic dangers of natural asset depletion 'resource management', unlike 'frontier economics', advocates the calculation and incorporation of environmental costs and benefits into national accounts; Aecology is being economized (Colby 1990, p. 23). The interdependence of ecosystems is recognised, along with the need to maintain both ecological processes and natural capital stocks as the basis for sustainable growth. Policies advocated include energy efficiency, general resource conservation, ecosystem monitoring and 'the polluter pays' principle in order to internalise the social costs of pollution. Price incentives are also seen as a major tool for encouraging sustainable environmental practices. The discipline of environmental economics is becoming well-established but Brazilian economists have not yet seriously addressed national or regional ecological problems in these terms except in a very general fashion (Pearce 1989; Margulis 1990). The Brazilian State could certainly do much to introduce price and other incentives to encourage more sustainable resource-use in Amazonia, where the billions of dollars spent in pursuing 'frontier economics' strategies have, over the last three decades, so effectively subsidised destructive settlement practices.

If conservationism is the major environmental policy approach for Amazonia and economised, 'resource management' techniques are becoming more common, strains of the most recent paradigm, that of 'eco-development', are also emerging. Although various concepts of 'eco-development' have been advanced, it has recently been defined as 'reorganizing human activities so as to be synergetic with ecosystem processes and services (Colby 1990, p. 23). Thus, the environment is to be treated neither as a sink, nor simply as a resource under constant threat of over-exploitation to be carefully managed, but as the very basis for economic development. Sustainable development would therefore include 'steady-state' growth goals based on the following policy priorities (Colby 1990, Adams 1990): use of clean, renewable energy sources; meeting people's basic needs; participatory planning from the grassroots; the greater use of indigenous knowledge to define appropriate technologies; and the ecologically sound management of common property regimes. While open to accusations of being 'populist' and 'romantic' in many of its more far-fetched prescriptions, some 'eco-development' ideas are starting to form the basis of a new approach to environmental management in Amazonia. As we shall see, this is founded to a large extent on the power of socio-environmental grassroots movements to devise locale-specific, 'productive conservation' solutions; reconciling the twin, symbiotic goals of conserving natural resources while sustaining local livelihoods.

18

Socio-environmental movements as social actors

Deterministic, over-arching paradigms of social change such as Marxism, neo-Marxist dependency theory and functionalism are of limited use for the purpose of policy prescription. These are gradually being complemented, if not totally replaced, by a more 'actor-oriented' approach within a limited post-modernist framework, which recognises the power of groups to influence the outcomes of change processes. Although structural or basic characteristics may constitute a prerequisite for a given change path, they do not predetermine social patterns (Long 1988; Touraine 1988). Outcomes will depend heavily on the particular strategies devised and alliances formed by groups to deal with problems as they arise. Farmers, fisher people and other social actors are seen as '... "knowledgeable" and "capable". They attempt to solve problems, learn how to intervene in the flow of events around them' (Long and Long 1992, p. 23). Within this perspective, social movements are perceived as collective social actors and not as acquiescent instruments for executing predetermined historical tendencies. Correspondingly, the State apparatus is seen not as monolithic and totally impervious to bottom-up pressure. Rather, progressive State managers and sectors exist which are often responsive to popular appeals under certain conditions; especially when effective political force can be applied through social movements and other pressure groups.

Socio-environmental movements in Amazonia are most appropriately conceived within a 'resource mobilisation' framework (Hall 1997a). Such groups are seen essentially as rational-utilitarian, basing their strategies on calculations of likely material benefits and costs. Their actions involve conflicts of interest with the State and private sector arising from institutionalised power relations. Success in establishing a conservation strategy is judged by whether a given group becomes recognised as the legitimate representative of collective interests. However, in trying to justify the longer-run sustainability of movements, a neo-utilitarian approach, on its own, is insufficient. As Cohen (1985, p. 691) suggests, 'the logic of collective interaction entails something other than strategic or instrumental rationality'. As highlighted by Bates (1988) in his version of 'rational choice' theory, it is also necessary to consider other social features such as shared perceptions arising from common experiences and community solidarity. Scott's (1990, p. 6) definition captures this complexity and can be applied to the case discussed in this paper: 'A social movement is a collective actor constituted by individuals who understand themselves to have common interests and, for at least some significant part of their social existence, a common identity'.

Many of the features of social movements identified by Scott (1990) apply equally well to socio-environmental movements in Amazonia - as, indeed, elsewhere in the developing world. Such action may unify a diverse range of smaller groups at grassroots level, not necessarily on a social class basis, around a specific, common theme or threat to their livelihoods. The need for collective action is seen as a rational calculation and is necessitated by the failure of formal political channels to effectively represent people's interests and resolve the problems in question. Given the traditionally omissive stance of the police and judiciary, a collective response may well be the only option open to poorer and weaker groups in the face of a threatened invasion of their common property assets by outside interests. The existence of socio-environmental movements will depend on context-specific factors, both objective and subjective, internal to the group and also in terms of relationships established with other organisations.

Traditional models of common resource use are pessimistic with regard to their potential for conservation. Hardin's (1968) classic 'tragedy of the commons' argument, for example, suggests that individual self-interest will always outweigh collective interests in the use of common property, leading inevitably to resource over-exploitation and degradation. The 'prisoner's dilemma' game and 'logic of collective action' schools of thought also suggest that it is not possible to have strategies which are rational both collectively as well as individually (Ostrom 1990). The implication of these notions is that short-term, individual self-interest is the only inherently 'rational' form of human behaviour, and that this will, under all but very exceptional circumstances, override and undermine group interests.

Such theories have underpinned much environmental policy-making in Brazil and developing countries generally, with their emphasis on the command-and-control, protectionist strategies discussed above. The underlying assumption is that cooperation is impossible and that coercive force from central government, imposed from the outside, is always necessary in order to protect natural resource systems. This may be achieved either by means of a central authority taking direct charge of a resource system, or through government 'privatisation' of the resource; that is, by parcelling out ownership rights and allowing individuals to follow their own interests within a clearly defined set of property rights.

However, a clear distinction must be made between *open access regimes* which permit an uncontrolled free-for-all, and authentic *common property regimes (CPRs)*. In contrast to the former, the latter have 'structured ownership arrangements within which management rules are developed, group size is known and enforced, incentives exist for co-owners to follow the accepted institutional arrangements, and sanctions work to ensure compliance' (Bromley and Cernea 1989, p. iii). The fact that numerous examples of well-managed CPRs exist in various parts of the developing world, suggests that there is no inevitable tendency for people sharing a common resource to be automatically caught in a vicious circle of environmental degradation as individuals exclusively pursue their own interests. As Ostrom notes (1990, p. 21), 'some individuals have broken out of the trap inherent in the commons dilemma, whereas others continue remorsefully trapped into destroying their own resources'.

Following the 'actor-oriented' perspective discussed above, the underlying premise of this paper is that the ability of local communities with common pool resource problems to find solutions will vary considerably from situation to situation. It is argued here, however, that the existence of an active, locally-based socio-environmental movement is one of the strongest prerequisites which may enable CPR-dependent groups to play a decisive role in devising and applying resource system management plans. By adopting certain tactics and establishing alliances with key outsiders, including the State apparatus, such movements have become an increasingly critical force for productive conservation in Brazilian Amazonia. In the absence of such grassroots organisation and pressure, it is highly unlikely that solutions for balanced CPR use will be found which successfully reconcile individual user interests with their collective benefit.

This paper will address two related questions: (i) What factors facilitate the emergence of a grassroots socio-environmental movement? and (ii) Perhaps more importantly from the point of view of this discussion, in what specific ways can such movements assist in operationalising the concept of 'productive conservation'? In seeking answers to these questions, reference will be made to one particular emerging socio-environmental movement in Brazilian Amazon centred around the Mamirauá Ecological Station in western Amazonia, which is currently engaged in a process of devising a management strategy for its extractive, common resource system.

Mobilisation for productive conservation

As already stressed, attempts at devising strategies for productive conservation are far more likely to be successful if they are founded upon an active socio-environmental movement. This plays several important roles both in generating the initial impetus for collective action over CPR regulation as well as in providing a strong basis for the longer-run sustainability of a management strategy. These crucial roles will be illustrated with reference to Mamirauá.

The Fisher people of Lake Mamirauá: background [3]

The best-known social movement for natural resource conservation in Amazonia is undoubtedly that of the rubber tappers of Acre, Rondônia and Amapá states.[4] However, this paper will focus on another more recent instance of popular mobilisation which, although at a relatively embryonic stage and more localised that the rubber tappers, holds promise as a potential model for productive conservation of fish resources in the rich floodplains or *várzeas* of Amazonia.

The Mamirauá Ecological Station, formally established in 1990, comprises 1.1 million hectares of whitewater (nutrient-rich), seasonally flooded rainforest, situated between the Rivers Solimões and Japurá, just north of the city of Tefé in Amazonas state. It is extremely rich in biodiversity with a high degree of endemism, supporting six species of primates, many bird species and an abundance of aquatic animals and commercially valuable fish such as the *tambaquí* and *pirarucú*. The local economy is based on fishing in the rivers, lakes and cut-off channels which form during the dry season (low-water) periods, as well as on subsistence farming, timber extraction and minor forest products. Inhabitants do not have land titles, since all *várzea* lands are formally the property of the navy, but squatter laws allow usufruct rights to be acquired. Most of the *várzea*, with its stocks of fish and timber, is effectively a common property resource.

Reserve inhabitants fish for subsistence needs and local sale using a variety of low-volume techniques. However, in recent years fish stocks at Mamirauá have been endangered by the penetration of large-scale commercial fishing boats coming from as far away as Manaus, which use high-volume extraction and refrigeration methods. Indeed, the problem of predatory commercial fishing endangering the livelihoods of fisher people has become a serious one along the whole middle stretch of the River Amazon.

The idea of turning Mamirauá into a protected Ecological Station was first proposed in 1984 by a Brazilian primatologist, Dr.Márcio Ayres, who had been carrying out research in the area. With support from the Brazilian government as well as foreign donors, attempts are currently underway to design and implement a management plan with the active participation of the local population. Conservation efforts are presently concentrated in the focal area of 200,000 hectares, which is used by 50 riverine communities with about 4,500 inhabitants, largely *caboclos*[5] and some Amerindians. An NGO, the *Sociedade Civil Mamirauá*, has been set up to run the programme, which is divided into several sub-components dealing with core operations, scientific research, socio-economic research and extension activities. The aim of the exercise is to reconcile biodiversity conservation with the collective, sustainable use of the reserve's natural resources (fish and timber). A management plan has been produced which includes zoning for subsistence, commercial and restocking purposes, the design of conservation and protection measures, scientific research to provide the required information on aquatic and terrestrial resource systems, as well as setting up health, nutrition and environmental education programmes (Mamirauá 1996).

Mamirauá's population has for a many years been aware of the creeping assault on the fish stocks of the reserve area. As will be detailed below communities have, supported by the local Catholic church, been actively resisting outside incursions by commercial fishing vessels since the 1970s, although in a rather sporadic and disorganised fashion. The project marks a new phase in this process by attempting for the first time in the *várzeas* of Brazilian Amazonia to implement a durable and integrated management plan for productive conservation, building upon these early initiatives of the local population to protect their livelihoods and its common property base.

Organising for conservation at Mamirauá

Socio-environmental movements share certain features and perform a variety of roles in terms, firstly, of enhancing the countervailing power of communities defending their CPRs as well as, secondly, in longer-run, systematic resource management. Before discussing these specific

23

attributes, however, it is worth briefly considering the those features which are preconditions for the emergence of a SEM.

In those relatively few Amazonian natural resource common property systems where socio-environmental movements have been successfully organised, certain structural conditions prevail which favour, but do not guarantee, the emergence of grassroots activity. These conditions apply to Mamirauá and may be broken down as follows.

Group identity Resource-users, whether farmers, forest extractivists or fisher people (or a combination of these), form a clearly identifiable group in terms of their main activity and the geographical area occupied. The *vargueiros* (as users of the *várzea* are known) of Mamirauá do form such a well-defined group in terms of their economic activities and vested interest in the natural resources in question. This is despite the existence of some divisions due to geographical isolation caused by vertical, river-based lines of communication, religious beliefs (Catholic vs Protestant communities) and cultural backgrounds (*caboclo* and Amerindian).

CPR-based livelihoods They share a strong motivation to preserve natural resources because these form the mainstay of the group's livelihood. Economic and ecological considerations thus become inextricably linked. Although subsistence agriculture is widespread at Mamirauá, fish is the most important staple and commercial product, along (increasingly) with timber in certain areas.

Interdependence Furthermore, resource system users do not exist in isolation from each other. As the pressure on natural assets grows, there is an increasing degree of interdependence amongst users which may provide the stimulus for cooperation in their utilisation. Prior activity by change agents such as the Church and NGOs in a given area often serves to hasten this process. Such collaboration has become increasingly evident at Mamirauá as the project has evolved over past several the years.

Resources threatened After years of relatively untroubled existence, users suddenly find their natural resource base under attack from predatory incursions by outsiders whose practices threaten the sustainability of the renewable resource base. At Mamirauá, this danger has come mainly from external, commercial fishing boats, but also exists internally from CPR users themselves invading forbidden areas reserved for restocking.

Given these basic preconditions, a local movement may organise for productive conservation in a number of ways, ranging from immediate defence of their natural resource system to longer-term cooperation, both amongst themselves and with outside organisations, for developing a resource management strategy.

Self-defence

Direct threats from outside forces are often the catalyst for concerted action by groups in their own self-defence, by means of which a hitherto relatively fragmented and weak population can become a source of countervailing power against traditionally much stronger groups. This may take two forms, over the short- and long-term respectively.

Initial resistance During the early stage of the CPR movement, the capacity to quickly mobilise people means that user groups can mount immediate resistance, physically preventing outsiders from stealing their resources. Such action invariably helps to generate a stronger sense of community spirit which serves as a constructive base for more prolonged community involvement in monitoring and planning activities. During the 1970s in the Mamirauá-Tefé region, grassroots action generally increased as a result of activities pursued by the *Movimento de Ecucação de Base* (MEB), the Prelacy of Tefé and its adoption of Liberation Theology and the new rural trades union. Emulating the rubber tappers, fisher people of the region carried out aquatic *empates*[6] against commercial fishing vessels, but in a disorganised fashion and with no proper strategy. This kind of struggle has for several years been typical of many fishing communities along River Solimões and mid-reaches of the River Amazon. At Mamirauá, however, this grassroots strength has been built upon to mount a policing scheme for the CPR as the basis for a long-term conservation plan.

Long-term policing At a later stage, this capacity for collective action can be harnessed to provide more structured, continuous policing and monitoring operations, usually with some outside assistance, to enforce management rules. At Mamirauá, a system of permanent vigilance by *vargueiros* has been set up. Lakes for fishing and preservation have been signposted, a series of floating guard posts equipped with short-wave radios have been placed at strategic lake entrance points, and a system of radio communications has been established between the project and IBAMA

25

headquarters to quickly report infractions. Some communities have already taken the initiative to 'close off' certain lakes to outsiders. Although the Mamirauá project has funded vital equipment and staffing costs, the system could not function without the comprehensive vigilance of the community in its policing role.

Conservation strategy

A local movement can also represent the interests of CPR users during the invariably long drawn-out process of designing and implementing an appropriate management scheme for the particular resource system in question. This is crucial, given the need to devise situation-specific solutions in areas of high ecological diversity such as Amazonia. Blueprints imposed *a priori* from outside simply will not work, as has been demonstrated time and time again. Socio-environmental movements can, therefore, prove instrumental not just for territorial defence but also in the more effective planning of productive resource-use once CPRs are relatively secure. This transition is well underway at Mamirauá. The intensity of such contributions by local movements to this process will obviously vary depending on the circumstances of each case, ranging from minor involvement to playing a major role in project design. This may be achieved in a number of ways.

Information-gathering Designing an effective management strategy for the collective, non-destructive use of natural resources, especially in complex ecosystems such as Amazonia's, requires the collecting of much information. This may be necessary to establish very fundamental parameters such as the physical boundaries and natural features of the resource system, its human carrying capacity, the demographic and socio-economic structure and other base-line data for monitoring and evaluation purposes. At a more sophisticated stage of development, it may be necessary to calculate the benefits and costs of establishing such a strategy, in order to demonstrate to users the rationality of long-term productive conservation as opposed to short-run 'mining' of the environment. This information, if properly presented, could help overcome the 'free-rider' problem of CPR systems by advising resource users of the potential benefits of such a strategy.

Efficient information-gathering requires the full cooperation of the community with researchers through the use of rapid (RRA) and participatory rural appraisal (PRA) techniques (Chambers 1992). The task

26

of collecting data may be partly delegated to resource-users themselves following basic training. This is sometimes done in order to reduce the costs of data collection in view of the communications difficulties in resource systems covering huge geographical areas. It can also, however, be useful for gaining users confidence and as an educational and training mechanism for involving them in the process of planning and sustaining a management strategy to fit local circumstances.

At Mamirauá, the community played, and continues to play, a key role in helping natural and social scientists to gather the information necessary for the formulation of a long-term resource management plan. Although considered a 'softer' form of participation than policing, for example, this can nevertheless be an important management tool. Effective conservation must be guided by accurate data on the resource base and use patterns. Thus, community members cooperate with teams of researchers in the sub-programmes for aquatic and terrestrial systems investigations, as well as in socio-economic studies of community history and structure, and human migratory patterns. Following consultation with CPR users, in order to increase the more immediate flow of benefits to local people and to help unite the population, programmes of primary health care and environmental education are also being mounted by extension workers. Information about the on-going activities of the project is also shared at annual general assemblies of community representatives, as well as at local meetings.

Cost-sharing Although sometimes portrayed as the most rudimentary and passive form of community participation (Paul 1987), provision of resources by project beneficiaries can form a vital component in resource management, especially when combined with other forms of involvement. For example, CPR users are best placed to provide labour for defensive and policing activities, given their sheer presence on the ground and knowledge of local circumstances. This kind of operation is often very difficult for an environmental protection agency to undertake effectively, especially when lacking in political will and/or funding, as is often the case. At Mamirauá, as already mentioned, this kind of collaboration is critical to the success of the conservation strategy. Other forms of cost-sharing may also serve to demonstrate resource-users commitment to a conservation plan; such as contributions of food for community meetings and donations of construction materials for putting up basic infrastructure.

27

Negotiation and communal responsibility Potentially, the most critical role of CPR user organisations is that of negotiating or bargaining with government authorities over the design of the conservation area and the rights/obligations of those who utilise its resources. Such associations are becoming far more pro-active than in the past. Whereas previously they may have been content with a more passively participatory role in terms of cost-sharing and limited consultation, for example, nowadays there is a marked trend for local organisations to become more aggressive in the face of threats to their natural resource base and to demand a more vigorous involvement in project planning. Ultimately, such pressure may bring about significant policy reforms, as in the case of the rubber-tappers with the creation of Extractive Reserves.

At Mamirauá, negotiation and bargaining have been necessary both internally amongst various interested parties, as well as externally between the project as a whole and State agencies. A system of democratic representation of interests was set up through which elected community members meet regularly at village, local (sectoral) and CPR-wide (general assembly) levels. *Vargueiros* themselves, guided and assisted by scientists using research data, have undertaken zoning exercise to designate areas for subsistence, commercial and preservation purposes. Six categories of lake use were established by CPR users at community meetings, and each geographical sub-sector (of which there are nine) was responsible for classifying and zoning the areas under their influence as part of the management plan. In addition to dealing with incursions by larger fishing vessels, inter-communal negotiation has also had to face the problem of illicit fishing by CPR users themselves. A system of vigilance, warnings and sanctions has also been devised to address this sensitive problem.

Thus, the exercise in participatory zoning will, it is hoped, help generate a sense of CPR-wide communal responsibility amongst both *vargueiros* as well as smaller commercial fisher people servicing local towns, which have traditionally been supplied by Lake Mamirauá. This should go a long way towards solving the 'commons dilemma' of reconciling individual and collective concerns in resource conservation, although some conflicts of interest are bound to persist.

Alliances Socio-environmental movements on their own, no matter how well-organised or how vociferous, often have rather limited power. Their potential is most effectively tapped when they can form strategic alliances with outside organisations that wield political influence, at domestic and/or international level. There is often a wide variety of influential outside actors in such situations; progressive State managers in key central and regional or local government institutions, the radical Catholic church, rural trades unions, non-governmental organisations (NGOs), universities and other research agencies as well as official aid donors, both bilateral and multilateral. In the case of Mamirauá, such alliances have allowed sporadic protest to become organised into an effective socio-environmental movement for resource conservation. This has not involved the intense international political lobbying which characterised the rubber-tappers' campaign, for example, but this combination of forces has been instrumental in enabling the conservation strategy to be implemented.

In the Brazilian context, the radical Catholic church has played a crucial role in organising grassroots religious communities (*comunidades eclesiais de base* - CEBs). Based on a combination of Freirian methods and Liberation Theology, CEBs have been major channels for development project funding and incipient human rights and social protest movements, particularly during the 1970s when political opposition in Brazil was effectively banned (Hall 1993b). The activities of many committed rural trades unions (*Sindicatos de Trabalhadores Rurais* - STRs) and local associations are often based on earlier (and continuing) CEB involvement on the part of community members. As mentioned above, these alliances were particularly important in helping the *vargueiros* to defend their fish reserves during the 1980s, before the conservation project existed.

NGOs, both national and overseas, have been of crucial importance in a number of ways, both politically and instrumentally. Strong lobbying by US and European environmental groups, for example, has had a significant impact on decisions by the Brazilian government to undertake policy reform in Amazonia; for example, in the case of Extractive Reserves. Alliances between local movements and NGOs are also vital in terms of providing the funding and operational skills which outside organisations can bring to bear on the challenge of designing and implementing CPR management plans. The World Wildlife Fund (WWF) and Wildlife Conservation International (WCI) have provided substantial funding.

The Goeldi Museum and Federal University of Pará in Belém have provided institutional backing for the project's two founder members, who themselves have constituted an NGO to administer the scheme, the *Sociedade Civil Mamirauá*, with offices in Tefé and Belém. The project has received major backing from Brazil's National Council for Science and Technology (CNPq) and Ministry of the Environment (MMA), and falls under the jurisdiction of the Environment Institute (IMA) of Amazonas state. The British Overseas Development Administration (ODA, now the Department for International Development - DfID) is the largest foreign donor to the project. With the growing decentralisation of environmental controls in Brazil, the influence of local and state-level authorities is becoming increasingly important in this question. Seven municipalities in this region, including Tefé, have decreed that *empates* against invading outside commercial fishing boats are a legally valid tactic by means of which local communities may defend their fish stocks (*Jornal do Brasil* 1994).

Conclusion

This paper has tried to demonstrate how, at the level of project design and execution, well-organised grassroots action can make a major contribution towards and indeed, constitute the foundation of, a long-term CPR management strategy. Although this process is still in its infancy at Mamirauá, progress to date augurs well for the future. The project has been decreed a 'Sustainable Development Reserve' under Amazonas state law, pending the revision of legislation of Conservation Units to allow the inclusion of productive conservation initiatives such as this one (Hall 1997b).[7] If successful, therefore, the Mamirauá experience could form the basis of a new model of natural resource conservation for a much larger area of *várzea* along the rivers Amazon and Solimões, where fishing communities face similar problems of protecting their common property rights.

At one level, the challenge is to turn a virtually open access system, with its inherent threat of degradation, into one that is controlled and managed in the interests of its users to simultaneously protect biodiversity and livelihoods.

Yet the repercussions of projects such as Mamirauá are far wider repercussions, for they have played an important role in persuading decision-makers that an alternative approach to environmental management in Amazonia is indeed feasible if appropriate support is forthcoming. Under such pioneering influences, policy-making for Amazonia has evolved and matured to the extent that notions of sustainability and community involvement in resource management have become an integral part of official policy, as reflected in Brazil's *Integrated National Policy for the*

Legal Amazon (Brazil 1995) and *Agenda 21 for Amazonia* (Brazil 1997). Notwithstanding any element of rhetoric as well as the many obstacles to implementing such policies, this is undoubtedly a major step forward. It can safely be said that, through socio-environmental movements, natural resource-users in Amazonia are beginning to have a profound impact at all levels on the circumstances which affect their livelihoods and physical environments.

Notes

1. Senior Lecturer in Social Planning in Developing Countries, Department of Social Policy and Administration, London School of Economics and Political Science, Houghton Street, London WC2A 2AE. Email: <a.l.hall@lse.ac.uk>. The author would like to thank Dr.Márcio Ayres and Dr. Deborah Lima of the Mamirauá project for their assistance in facilitating the fieldwork upon which this chapter is based.

2. Successive military and civilian governments have since 1964 pursued a range of policies aimed at settling and 'integrating' the region, which comprises 60 per cent of the country, into the national economy. The strategies chosen for achieving these objectives have invariably been based on complementary geopolitical and profit-maximizing aims, with little consideration of the huge social and environmental, not to mention financial, costs thus incurred (Goodman and Hall 1990). Livestock development, encouraged by tax breaks and other subsidies amounting to over US$ one billion have left a legacy of severely degraded pasture lands and largely failed enterprises (Gasques and Yokomizo 1985; Mahar 1988). Highway construction across the region and government propaganda have encouraged the uncontrolled in-migration of hundreds of thousands of poor farmers from the drought-stricken North-East and from the increasingly mechanised rural South. Small farmer settlement on officially sponsored settlement projects along the Transamazon highway (the road cost an estimated US2.3 billion to build), and later in the North-Western states of Rondonia and Acre, have fuelled this trend (Smith 1982; Martine 1990; Bakx 1990). Peasant farmers have entered into conflict with large individual and corporate landed interests, and failed colonists have been forced to abandon INCRA schemes through lack of government support. Land-titling and agrarian reform legislation have further encouraged settlers to cut down the forest as proof of ownership and 'productive use', while commercial logging in Amazonia is on the increase (Hall 1990; Schneider 1992). Large mining and infrastructural developments such as the Carajás complex have further stimulated in-migration by workers and farmers in search of jobs (Hall 1989; Redwood 1993). Thus, a combination of cattle ranching, small farmer

settlement, logging, mining and land speculation have been responsible for the estimated 12 per cent level of deforestation in Brazilian Amazonia, which rises to 30-40 per cent in the most heavily settled areas of southern Pará and Rondônia.

3. Information in this paper on the Mamirauá Ecological Station has been derived from field visits by the author as well as Lima Ayres (1993) and Faulhaber (1987).

4. Following years of violent confrontation between rubber tappers and cattle ranchers, culminating in the death of Francisco 'Chico' Mendes in 1988, pressure from the National Council of Rubber Tappers (CNS) along with a powerful international and domestic NGO lobby movement, succeeded in bringing about the creation in 1990 of a new concept under Brazilian law; that of the 'Extractive Reserve'. To date, four such reserves have been officially created covering 2.2 million hectares with a population of some 22,000 people. Another five, already in existence, will be decreed covering a similar area. The extractive reserve movement has succeeded in attracting funding from a range of bilateral, multilateral and non-governmental donor agencies, most recently under the 'G-7 Pilot Programme to Conserve the Brazilian Rainforest' (Brazil 1992).

5. *Caboclos* are mixed-race descendants of indigenous, white Portuguese and black populations.

6. The *empate* or 'stand-off' is a technique which has since 1980 been successfully employed by the rubber tappers of Acre and Rondônia to prevent illicit cutting down of rubber trees by cattle ranchers and commercial loggers. This involves confrontations by large groups of men, women and children in which rubber tappers would use minimum force necessary to stop labourers deforesting the areas in question. Fisher people in the mid-Amazon region have used similar tactics to chase off outside fishing vessels and sometimes temporarily seize the boats to hand over to the authorities.

7. The legal category of 'Ecological Station' does not permit the extraction of resources at all, in principle, but it was the best option available at the time which would allow protective measures to be implemented.

References

Adams, W. (1990), *Green Development: Environment and Sustainability in the Third World*, Routledge, London.

Bakx, K. (1990), 'The Shanty Town, Final Stage of Rural Development?' in Goodman and Hall, pp. 49-69.

Bates, R. (ed.) (1988), *Towards a Political Economy of Development*, University of California Press, Berkeley.

Branford S. and Glock, O. (1985), *The Last Frontier: Fighting Over Land in the Amazon*, Zed, London.

Brazil (1992), *Projeto Reservas Extrativistas*, Programa Piloto para Preoptic das Florestas Tropicais Brasileiras, Brasília.

Brazil (1995), *Integrated National Policy for the Amazon-Brazil*, Ministry of the Environment, Brasilia.

Brazil (1997), *Agenda 21 for Amazonia*, Ministry of the Environment, Brasilia.

Bromley, D. and Cernea, M. (1989), 'The Management of Common Property Resources: Some Conceptual and Operational Fallacies', *World Bank Discussion Paper*, 57, World Bank, Washington, D.C.

Brundtland Commission (1987), *Our Common Future*, Oxford University Press, Oxford.

Chamber, R. (1992), 'Rural Appraisal: Rapid, Relaxed and Participatory', *Discussion Paper*, 311, Institute of Development Studies, University of Sussex, Brighton.

Cohen, J. (1985), 'Strategy or Identity: New Theoretical Paradigms and Contemporary Social Movements', *Social Research*, Vol.52, No.4, pp. 663-7116.

Colby, M. (1990), 'Environmental Management in Development: The Evolution of Paradigms', *World Bank Discussion Paper*, 80, World Bank, Washington D.C.

Faulhaber, P. (1987), *O Navio Encantado: Etnia e Alianças em Tefé*, Museo Paraense Emílio Goeldi, Belém.

Furley, P. (1990), 'The Nature and Sustainability of Brazilian Amazon Soils', in Goodman and Hall, pp. 309-359.

Gasques, J. and Yokomizo, C. (1985), 'Avaliação dos Incentivos Fiscais na Amazônia', *mimeo.*, IPEA, Brasília.

Goodman, D. and Hall, A., eds. (1990), *The Future of Amazonia: Destruction or Sustainable Development?* Macmillan, London.

Hall, A. (1989), *Developing Amazonia: Deforestation and Social Conflict in Brazil's Carajás Programme*, Manchester University Press, Manchester.

Hall, A. (1990), 'Land Tenure and Land Reform in Brazil', in R. Prosterman, M. Temple and T. Hanstead, eds. *Agrarian Reform and Grassroots Development*, Lynne Rienner, Boulder & London, pp. 205-232.

Hall, A. (1993a), 'Making People Matter: Sociology and Development in Brazilian Amazonia', *International Journal of Contemporary Sociology*, Vol.30, No.1, pp. 63-80.

Hall, A. (1993b), 'Non-Governmental Organisations and Development in Brazil Under Dictatorship and Democracy', in C. Abel and C. Lewis, eds., *Welfare, Poverty and Development in Latin America*, Macmillan, London, pp. 421-437.

Hall, A. (1997a), *Sustaining Amazonia: Grassroots Action for Productive Conservation*, Manchester University Press, Manchester.

Hall, A. (1997b), 'Peopling the Environment: A New Agenda for Research, Policy and Action in Brazilian Amazonia', *European Review of Latin American and Caribbean Studies*, 62, June, pp. 9-31.

Hardin, G. (1968), 'The Tragedy of the Commons', *Science*, No.162, pp. 1243-1248.

Jornal do Brasil (1994), *'Empate' é lei de preservação em 7 municípios amazônicos*, 27 February.

Lima Ayres, D. (1993), 'A Implantação de Uma Unidade de Conservação em Área de Várzea: A Experiência de Mamirauá', *mimeo*.

Long, N. (1988), 'Sociological Perspectives on Agrarian Development and State Intervention', in A. Hall and J. Midgley, (eds.), *Development Policies: Sociological Perspectives*, Manchester University Press, Manchester.

Long, N. and Long, A., (eds.) (1992), *Battlefields of Knowledge*, Routledge, London.

Mahar, D. (1988), *Government Policies and Deforestation in Brazil's Amazon Basin*, World Bank, Washington D.C.

Mamirauá (1996), *Mamirauá: Plano de Manejo*, Sociedade Civil Mamirauá, Brasilia.

Margulis, S., (ed.) (1990), *Meio Ambiente: Aspectos Técnicos e Econômicos*, IPEA, Brasília.

Martine, G. (1990), 'Rondônia and the Fate of Small Producers', in Goodman and Hall, pp. 23-48.

Nogueira-Neto, P. (1992), *Ecological Stations: A Saga of Ecology and Environmental Policy*, Empresa das Artes, São Paulo.

Ostrom, E. (1990), *Governing the Commons: The Evolution of Institutions for Collective Action*, Cambridge University Press, Cambridge.

Paul, S. (1987), 'Community Participation in Development Projects: the World Bank Experience', *World Bank Discussion Paper*, 6, World Bank, Washington D.C.

Pearce, D., Markandya, A. & Barbier, E. (1989), *Blueprint for a Green Economy*, Earthscan, London.

Redwood, J. (1993), *World Bank Approaches to the Environment and Development: A Review of Selected Projects*, Operations Evaluation Department, World Bank, Washington D.C.

Schneider, R. (1992), 'Brazil: An Analysis of Environmental Problems in the Amazon', *mimeo.*, World Bank, Washington D.C.

Scott, A. (1990), *Ideology and the New Social Movements*, Unwin Hyman, London.

Smith, N. (1992), *Rainforest Corridors: The Transamazon Colonization Scheme*, University of California Press, Berkeley.

Touraine, A. (1988), *Return of the Actor*, University of Minnesota Press, Minneapolis.

3 Statelessness, Ethnicity and Conflict: Poverty-Focused Rural Development in Somalia 1991-1994

JOSEPH MULLEN

Introduction

This paper will analyse the empirical realities of the cycle of empowerment - powerlessness for poor communities within the historical context of the complex emergency of Somalia 1991-1994. It will examine the decline of vibrant communities racked by war and ethnic conflict and the tentative piecing together of shattered local policies against a broader background of United Nations armed and humanitarian interventions. An interesting corollary which runs contrary to received wisdom on central-local relations is that ethnicity emerges as an ambivalent factor which simultaneously empowers within the context of the exercise of power through traditional forms of governance against the background of a disintegrated state, while on the other hand the vacuum of power created by the collapse of a central state is filled by ethnic-based violence in which vulnerability, destruction of the natural resource base of livelihood security and forced migration emerge as key characteristics. The role of NGOs and aid agencies is studied in this context. In conclusion, one surveys the fragility of empowerment which is characterised by an exposure to vulnerability, ethnicity and collapse of civil society. What emerges of critical importance is the shared ideological commitment which feeds into a shared value system and community solidarity. This underpins the emphasis on communal concerns, overriding personal interest and individualism, which runs contrary to the western version of empowerment and presents an alternative basis for sustainability.

More specifically, this paper will also assess the socio-political framework within which a transition from relief to rehabilitation could have been possible and various institutional delivery mechanisms for agricultural producers, with a view to restoring production capacity. In this latter context, the results of a rapid rural appraisal at village level in war-torn areas will be discussed. The role of local councils will be considered and how these could have intermeshed with a scaled down, highly decentralised regional administration. The contribution of NGOs and their potential role in collaborating with and legitimising traditional institutions will be discussed.

Background to the conflict

The unitary state of Somalia, since the fall of Siad Barré in January 1991, no longer exists de facto; there is no central government which can claim legitimacy or recognition by all stakeholders. Five major militia groupings dominated various regions of the country, mainly on the basis of clan alliances. North-West Somalia (former British Somaliland), under the leadership of 'President' Tour, made a unilateral declaration of independence, established Ministries, but has neither resources nor recognition. In addition to the fragmentation of the state and the total collapse of public administration, a series of crippling catastrophes have befallen Somalia. Droughts over three seasons have exacerbated falling production levels attributable to inter and intra clan warfare, population dislocation, massive loss of life and looting of animal stocks and seasonal food reserves. It is estimated that 300,000 Somalis have died from hunger-related diseases, close to 100,000 as the result of armed conflict and 700,000 Somalis fled the country as refugees. As many more have been displaced. Public infrastructure has been demolished; scientific institutions such as agricultural research stations and part of the University have been destroyed. In certain instances, 50 years of documented research knowledge has been lost. Public libraries, government archives and the National Museum have befallen the same fate as the buildings in which they were housed. Virtually all public institutions associated with government - even those of a development nature such as dams, power plants, irrigation networks, wells or extension offices - have been destroyed or looted by armed bandits. The entire banking system ceased to operate and its resources have been plundered. Highly qualified Somalia personnel; engineers, agronomists, veterinarians and researchers have either left the country, are unemployed or are attached to aid organisations. Years of civil war, followed by factional fighting, have created extensive social upheaval. It is estimated that 1.5

million persons remain at great risk and perhaps three times that number require some form of assistance. In December 1992, under Security Council resolution 794, in an unprecedented intervention in the internal affairs of a member country, an American-led Unified Task Force (UNITAF), entered Somalia. The forces moved to secure the major ports, roads, provincial centre and airports. They then spread out into the major urban centres of Central and Southern Somalia. The eventual participation of a further 37 nations in the military operation and the internalisation of the military command structure led to a stronger integration of the military operation into the United Nations as the name United Nations Operations in Somalia (UNOSOM II) suggests.

UNOSOM operated both a civilian administration and a military operation simultaneously. Of the estimated USD 1.5 billion budget for one year of UNOSOM's operations, for both military and humanitarian, about one third of the overall figure was earmarked for humanitarian work to be carried out by the Division of Humanitarian Relief and Rehabilitation (DHRR). However, a clash of interests often existed between the military objectives and the humanitarian. In consequence the local Somali population, who were often been alienated by the military activities of UNOSOM, found it difficult to extend legitimacy to UNOSOM's humanitarian activities. There were close linkages between the military operations and humanitarian initiatives - which may explain the lack of sustainability of UNOSOM's political and humanitarian initiatives after withdrawal and the UN failure to negotiate an agreed settlement or establish the legitimacy of the state.

The proposed national institutional framework for a new Somalia

The sole legislative blueprint for a future Somalia was the Draft Transitional Charter which is a UNOSOM inspired document worked out in consultation with local political and clan leaders. Reactions of the militia groupings have to the TNC are divided essentially on the issue of a centralised state. General Mohammed Farah Aydeed (from the sub-clan Habar Gedir) agreed on the concept but it was opposed by Ali Mahdi, the nominal President from the Abgal sub-clan. This fundamental difference of opinion between the two main parties relating to the role of a central state, compounded by sub-clan politics, continues to be a major destabilizing force in Somalia and is the basis of the current territorial division of the country. We shall now review the administrative aspects of decentralisation put forward by the

Charter, on the basis of which we shall then outline a village development institutional strategy.

The transitional National Council (TNC)

The TNC which could have acted as an interim National Assembly, drew its membership of the deputies from the 18 regions and 15 political movements in the country. It was intended to be the 'prime political authority having legislative functions during the transitional period' (Art 15). Simultaneously it would 'oversee the performance of departments created' and 'introduce a free market economy' (Art 15) based on private initiative which 'shall be free and unrestricted' (Art 8.3).

The Draft Transitional Charter did not distinguish clearly the division between national and regional functions, but, by inference, the primary national responsibility would be 'foreign affairs, national defence, post and telecommunications, sea, air and land transport, foreign trade, finance and any other areas so defined by law' (Art 39). It was assumed that, by default, the development functions of Agriculture, Health, Education and Local Government would be decentralised to the regional levels. In relation to Agricultural Sector institutions, only matters of national interest would be located in a central Department; all other functions would be decentralised to the Regional and District levels.

Significantly, the response of the major militias to the TNC has been to move away from a concept of 18 regions, the administrative units established under the Siad Barré regime and to view the areas that they control militarily as the appropriate sub-national units, which substantially coincide with five geographical zones and reflect clan alliances. Even the self-proclaimed 'Republic of Somaliland' showed interest in a federal solution which could have allowed a substantial degree of regional autonomy. In the next section we shall analyse the implications of decentralisation in the Somali context.

Decentralisation as a strategy for rural development

Decentralisation is understood in classic administrative terms as the transfer of authority to plan, make decisions and manage public functions from the national level to the sub-national; be it regional, district or village. One may distinguish four forms of decentralisation depending upon the substantive content of the powers being transferred (see Rondinelli, 1993):

(i)   Deconcentration: the transfer of functions within a central government hierarchy from the centre to the field level;

(ii)   Delegation: the transfer of functions from central government to a parastatal agency or development authority, which exercises the function on behalf of central government;

(iii) Devolution: the transfer of functions from central government to autonomous sub-national government e.g. state, region or district, who discharges the function without a relationship of hierarchical accountability to the central state in a system of parallel authorities.

(iv)   Transfer to Non-Government Organisations (NGOs); responsibility for specific planning functions or delivery of public services, with varying degrees of management accountability, transferred from the state to non-governmental organisations, generally for a specific time period. Privatisation could also be included under this category.

Application of decentralisation to the Somali context

Problems arise when these concepts are applied to Somalia; the reference to a central state is redundant as one does not currently exist in Somalia. While certain functions may fall, de jure, within the remit of central government, de facto every function which a regional or district government authority can satisfactorily implement is there for the taking. In the existing vacuum of statelessness, the power of legitimate local government comes from the community upwards rather than the top-down flow implied in conventional decentralisation. Power comes from a unique combination of clan or sub-clan alliances, legitimacy of traditional authorities and the barrel of a gun.

A powerful argument for local and regional government lies in its potential to shift resources out of the centre to the local level so the delivery of services to the rural poor is more effective and beneficiaries become empowered through participating in the design and management of rehabilitation programmes. This is particularly relevant to Somalia of today where human dignity has been severely damaged as a result of powerlessness and vulnerability in the face of drought, disaster and military excesses. The humiliating experience of feeding centres and food hand-outs now requires a more positive development approach in partnership and reconstruction. In the absence of a central authority, a unique opportunity presents itself for bodies of elders, in collaboration with NGOs where appropriate, to be the basic unit of interface with the local farming community. This community based approach synchronises with locally adapted farmer-based research and extension systems, low import content technology, sustainable development systems, locally managed soil and water conservation systems and farmer-based marketing associations.

Role of the Council of Elders

A permanent feature in a changing Somali landscape is the role of Somali communities. Traditionally the community of elders discussed the major issues of governance confronting village communities, such as cultivation rights, water access, social harmony and domestic issues. With the demise of a central government these councils of elders have become more active and have played a key negotiating role with clan-based militias. Although the councils of elders are not formally constituted bodies and they function on 'when needed' basis, they represent the most resilient and sustainable institution which incorporates both popular representation and legitimacy. The Council of Elders should have been given a central constitutional role in community self-management and not be considered as a 'stop-gap' solution in a situation of an institutional void, but have a strategic role to play in the regeneration of agricultural production and village life in general. A particular advantage of these councils is that they are grounded in cultural practices and enjoy local legitimacy. In fact, they have often played constructive intermediary roles with local militia in conflict resolution and in assuring the physical safety of NGO personnel.

In conclusion, in the short to medium term, in the absence of a legitimate central government, the assumption of functions by regional, district and village level authorities and to non-governmental organisations appears to be the most rational and indeed the only available option at this moment in time. A long term perspective might look towards a degree of centralisation of technical services consistent with a stronger central state. The administrative format is moving closer towards a 'devolutionary' model based on federalism between five regions, which could also perhaps include Somaliland.

The market environment

The draft Charter for the TNC affirms unambiguously its adherence to free market principles (Art 15) and an entrepreneurial spirit of private initiatives (Art 8). However, the linkages between rhetorical statements of market liberalisation and the actual conditions of producers and local markets are mediated through a series of variables, which include national and local security; supply of concessional food, status of infrastructure such as farm to market roads and port administration for export crops. These factors are given and emerged as key determinants in influencing market formation.

The free market is a central institution underpinning production and exchange. A free market is not however, established purely on the basis of a crude measure of supply and demand, which could constitute a highly imperfect market situation. It assumes that market prices reflect producer costs to maintain stability of supply; that a sense of security prevails to allow investment, raw material provision, production and marketing to take place. While supply and demand doubtlessly sets the market price for the exchange of goods currently in Somalia; the market could be described as imperfect in the extreme, particularly in relation to agricultural goods, because of the following distortions:

(i) the huge volume of concessional food imports and food in store lowered the market place of food below its actual production price. (Villagers interviewed in the Lower Somalia indicated that the open market price of maize was 60,000 shs while production costs were 80,000 shs see above). The same applied to locally produced seed;

(ii) the weak purchasing power of the local rural population in the wake of looting and destruction of capital and fixed assets;

(iii) the presence of numerous micro-markets, price variations varied from region to region, reflecting erratic supply, fluctuating demand, poor market information and lack of farm to market communications.

(iv) in certain areas, there is evidence of a breakdown of law and order and a collapse of customary duties and obligations regulating cultivation rights, water use and grazing areas.

Given the absence of a central financial or legislative authority, it is perhaps inevitable that supply and demand became the market norm. However, the situation represented a highly skewed and imperfect free market and increased the vulnerability of the dispossessed and marginalised.

Article 8 of the Transitional National Charter stated that the general economic policy shall be based on a free market. With the devolution of functions to the private sector, be it NGOs or commercial traders, the objective was full cost recovery for services rendered to farmers. It has, however, been the experience of many African countries, whose economies have been subjected to external shocks, that the recovery period has been

41

much longer than had at first been anticipated and that the most vulnerable in the population have required the protection of safety net measures and direct welfare transfers. In the case of Somalia where the shocks have been primarily endogenous and have resulted in the destruction of agricultural infrastructure, compounded by famine and civil war, substantial distortions have permeated the market environment. The terms of trade between animal production and crop production have moved in favour of the former by as much as a factor of three since the outbreak of hostilities. Both marketing and production networks are fragile, fragmented, highly localised and extremely vulnerable to changing micro-level security considerations. In many districts, the distinction between an emerging relief situation and rehabilitation was blurred. Therefore, it would not have been helpful in the short term to dogmatically oppose every form of concessionality in relation to agricultural inputs in the interests of shortening the transitional period from relief to rehabilitation. In all the village interviews the respondents confirmed categorically that they fully endorsed a free market without institutional controls but acknowledged that concessionality was needed in the interim. Weak market demand also constituted a major constraint.

Priorities identified for institutional action based on sustainability of village production systems

Introduction

In the absence of a central government all services to the population were carried out by international organisations such as United Nations agencies, notably UNHCR, UNDP, FAO and WFP, bilateral agencies or NGOs. The bulk of aid from 1991 - 1994 was relief. However, there was also a need to have a longer term vision of moving from relief into rehabilitation and strengthening the productive capacity of farmers so that basic food, clothing, potable water, health and education needs could be made accessible. The appropriate institutional delivery systems, in the absence of a central state, should therefore be strongly demand driven to ensure a modicum of sustainability. One stringent test of sustainability was to carry out a Participatory Rural Appraisal among the same communities as surveyed by the author six years earlier, with a number of the same informants. Village PRAs were undertaken in December 1993 in three regions of the country, revisiting a number of villages previously surveyed in 1987.

Village histories of conflict and incipient rehabilitation

Lower Shabelle: Aybuthe Village (close to Dar-es-Salaam) A meeting was held with 25 farmers at Aybuthe village (under the watchful eye of a platoon of Moroccan UNSOM troops!). The village of 430 households had been looted by retreating forces, all the food reserves were destroyed, the livestock were killed, even small chickens. People who resisted were shot down instantly (a similar incident was witnessed by the team that morning). Houses were burned and many people fled. All farm machinery including tractors, pumps and agricultural implements were looted. Slowly the people returned and for many this was their first season of cultivation. The Gu harvest was good but there was no market for the primary crop - maize - as the costs of production were actually higher than the selling price due to the large volumes of food aid in circulation, i.e. 80,000 shs per 100 kg, cost of production while 60,000 shs was the selling market price, a drop of 40 per cent on the pre-war price. Other problems related to marketing included the lack of security around Mogadishu which often resulted in roadside ambushes. If the market price of foodstuffs stabilised, the farmers stated they would be willing to purchase inputs on the open market. An improvement in security could have made it feasible to gain credit. Another priority was to rehabilitate silted up canals. The area under cultivation was less than half the pre-war level - and this has only been achieved thanks to the humanitarian aid when the people came back to their farms with nothing.

Bay Region: Asharfarta Village (near Baidoa) The village was a community-based production cooperative based on Islamic religious principles under the seminal leadership of the late Sheikh Banani, a local religious leader. The village represented a progressive agricultural community with an irrigation pump, high quality village housing, poultry raising, animal traction and trained village workers in agriculture, public health and education. Only one third of the harvest was used for domestic consumption, the remaining two thirds were split between local investment and sharing with other communities. Prior to the war the village boasted of 60 mango trees, 35 grapefruit trees, 120 heads of large livestock, 150 small livestock and 200 chickens. All were lost in the war and when the community returned 'there was not even shade to sit under', livestock had been slaughtered, trees destroyed and houses pillaged.

With the help of an NGO (Concern) the village restarted its production, albeit slowly. However, although it had only one acre of onions ready for harvesting, prices were so low that the price would not pay for the irrigation fuel bill.

The village leaders felt that agricultural credit is the way forward to rehabilitation. Credit would help to restock, draught animals, purchase inputs and stabilise the population. The marketing system is deemed to have collapsed. A village revolving fund for both investment and consumption was considered a priority.

Balmade Yakub Village The story as told by Mr Ibrahim Aden Nuur, Chief of Balmade Yakub Village in Bay Region is self explanatory:

> During the civil war Sayeed Barre's troops looted all of our property, we ran into the bush with some of our livestock which we killed and dried - this is what kept us alive. ICRC and Concern then opened field kitchens, they saved the lives of the children you see before you; we received clothing, food, seed and agricultural tools. We cannot just blame others. Some of our own people when they found their homes looted then proceeded to loot their neighbours if anything was left. Our rehabilitation priorities are implements and insecticide against leaf blight and a kind of emergency food bank.

Rice growing villages in Middle Shabelle - Jowhar An institutional review carried out by the author for the FAO (1987) singled out the rice growing villages of Middle Shabelle as examples of remarkable agricultural transformation and crop innovation. A German NGO, Agro Action, had played a catalytical role in this process. A comparison of acreage cultivated illustrates the dramatic drop in area cultivated:

Village	1987 No of ha	1993 No of ha
Banai	180	0
Kulundi	150	20
Barrei	100	0

The village of Banani, which was visited on foot under Italian military escort, was in a state of trauma. An elder put it 'we have lost our memory, we are unable to express ourselves properly, you are the first outsiders to come here since the war ended, please tell the world what our problems are'. Security remains a major preoccupation. 'Whatever we produce we are afraid that the soldiers or bandits will come back again and take it away from us; Nomads come with guns and graze their livestock on our cultivated fields, please have the guns collected, we are afraid to take any action'.

The elder continued 'heavy silting of canals is leading to flooding and water scarcity. Canals are being breached and water rota systems have disintegrated'. An old woman then stated gender-related concerns 'we women have suffered deeply in this war, our domestic lives are shattered and even simple cooking utensils have been stolen'.

The security situation remained extremely tense in both Middle and Lower Shabelle regions, social cohesion was under threat and local institutions for conflict resolution were under strain. In such a situation, it is difficult to know what form of social consensus could eventually emerge. Such an uncertain environment is inimical to medium or long term infrastructural investment and while market solutions to institutional provision of services may be a donor preferred option, these assume that a certain level of normality permit free exchange. In the short to medium term, the distinction between relief and rehabilitation will be blurred and a time frame to achieve market-based solutions should be flexible. Meantime, so as not to marginalise the vulnerable, exacerbate social differentials or exclude women from the development process, targeting and concessional input flows are essential to build up the capital base.

Issues arising from village consultations

Security The prioritisation of institutional services requested by farmers appeared to emphasise canal clearance (irrigated areas) traditional water conservation systems, e.g. in rainfed areas, a free market for goods, inputs, credit and extension services. But in all areas, security was perceived as a necessary prerequisite to profitable marketing. The risk premium charged by merchants was extremely high. Without incentives the response of farmers to produce surpluses in excess of the threshold of household food security was problematic. The production environment was further undermined by a breakdown of rotas among farmers for water access and armed clashes between agriculturalists and pastoralists over land use. A combination of these factors led to severe social tension, further population dislocation and a partial breakdown of farming systems.

An institutional response to this situation has various dimensions. At national level, agreement on the form of government would have created a clearly identifiable authority, which could restore social order in the countryside. However, the most immediate and perhaps effective solution was the Councils of Elders at local level to adjudicate disputes and impose socially acceptable sanctions. To address the issue of security of access to markets, farmers associations organised their own convoys, marketing and safe return of monies. The lack of any banking system meant that large sums of cash were constantly in circulation and an appreciating Somali shilling! The role of the emerging police force could have been expanded in to those activities although problems of acceptability were also in evidence. In the final analysis there will be a correlation between the level of security and the level of marketed crop surplus. The creation of a secure environment is dependent upon clan and sub-clan consensus, an enabling political system and supportive international partnerships. These three elements have not yet been brought together.

Marketing institutions When the choice of marketing arrangements were presented to the assembled farmers, representing about six villages in three regions, there was unanimity that production quotas and administered prices as practised under the former regime should not be restored under any shape or form. Despite the presence of fly-by-night traders and the risks of food shortages without buy-back options, the farmers were unequivocal about their preference for free marketing conditions without any state intermediaries.

The farmers, despite their stated preference for direct marketing in an uncontrolled environment, paradoxically, also expressed a concern for the maintenance of food buffer stocks to be held in reserve during the 'hungry' period and to act as an insurance against escalating food prices. This would involve a degree of intervention and a stabilising of market extremes. It is as if they quoted Dreze and Sen, 'Making room for private trade must not be confused with giving it an unrestrained and commanding influence on market operations when that influence has damaging effects on vulnerable people'.

Marketing food production and concessional food aid All the village communities consulted acknowledged the debt they owed to the distribution of food aid at a time when they were destitute. However, after two seasons of reasonably good rains in many areas, domestic surpluses built up but the marketing opportunities for these were limited. Food aid, therefore, had become a constraint on agricultural production.

Village communities in the Lower Shabelle, in particular, stated that the current market price of maize is 20 per cent cheaper than their actual production costs, substantially due to the fact that food aid flooded the market. While food aid is said to contribute to enhanced security and a decline in looting, it also, however, neutralises the production drive among local farming communities.

In this respect UNOSOM, as the coordinating agency of the relief and humanitarian effort, bore a substantial responsibility, in addition to the other food suppliers. It is indisputable that UNOSOM constituted the largest single source of purchasing power in the country with an annual budget of US$ 1.5 billion. Evidence suggests that their economic operations were primarily locked into international procurement and that the level of local procurement of goods and services and local economic integration was negligible. This huge purchasing power was therefore not generating any significant demand in the local economy (anecdotal evidence has suggested that UNOSOM even imported grapefruit, while quality fresh grapefruit were seen rotting on the market of Mogadishu while water melons were being exported). Although this may protect the local economy from excess demand, there were certain bridgeheads which could have been established without damaging local consumer interests. These could have included a procurement programme of food surplus for relief redistribution to food deficit areas, rather than having automatic recourse to external sources; the employment of local labour (labour was being imported from Kenya), and local procurement particularly of perishables such as fresh tropical fruits and meat (UNOSOM's property rental market benefited primarily members of the former regime and these rents were remitted overseas, creating little local demand). Furthermore, contracts for relief food and seed, such as maize and sorghum, could have been made with village associations and inputs provided in kind on a credit basis, to be recovered from the final price of the delivered product. Supply capacity had already been rehabilitated within local village economies to meet this demand.

Farmers Associations In order to reduce the vulnerability of individual subsistence farmers to security threats, particularly from armed bandits, in the procurement of inputs and the marketing of production, a strong case could be made for farmers associations at village level. These voluntary associations had the potential to agree on a common marketing strategy, manage food resources in times of emergency, organise secure storage systems and marketing logistics and liaise with aid agencies involved in food procurement and supply. As there was a major need to recapitalise farmers that have lost livestock, implements and inputs and whose livelihoods have been seriously threatened, the introduction of farmers savings and credit groups in the form of village revolving funds could have been particularly appropriate. In this respect, attention to the specific needs

47

of women and the rehabilitation of the domestic fabric of family life was considered a priority. NGOs could have played a central role in this local recovery and rehabilitation programme.

The role of NGOs At the height of the civil war in 1991-92, virtually all the major international and bilateral aid agencies moved their Somali operations to Nairobi. It was left to the NGOs remaining in Somalia to spearhead the humanitarian relief effort at great personal risk. They operated in a highly complex political situation, hired private security guards, arming them in certain instances, paying protection money and hoping to interpret correctly the shifting clan and sub-clan alliances. These bizarre practices were justified on the basis of clearing food supplies through the port, storage and distribution by road to up-country locations, where hunger and starvation was of monumental proportions. NGO efforts and media coverage contributed to the upsurge in public opinion which eventually led to international intervention. In all villages interviewed, appreciation was expressed by the people for the courage and effectiveness of NGOs in saving human life.

A principal reason justifying the intervention of UNITAF and subsequently UNOSOM II was the protection of the humanitarian aid effort. To some extent the price of protection may have been high in terms of loss of local political autonomy. NGO movements were substantially coordinated by UNOSOM II in daily logistic briefing for Mogadishu-based personnel by an American military officer in fatigues; and supplies were moved in convoys to up-country locations with heavily armed UN personnel in front and at the rear. There was less than efficient coordination between the different national military contingents responsible for the zones and most visits to villages were compulsorily carried out under military guard.

At any one time there were at least 93 NGOs collaborating under the broad umbrella of UNOSOM in Mogadishu, representing both the major international NGOs and small Somali NGOs. However, there was an unusually high level of Somali participation in the foreign NGOs, partly attributable to the hazardous security situation and the posting of senior personnel to Nairobi.

NGOs, typically, are thought to possess a number of organisational characteristics which give them a comparative advantage over government and international agencies in responding to crises and emergencies. They are said to exhibit a capability to respond quickly to situations, are less bureaucratic, make more effective use of their funds in reaching the poorest, encourage beneficiary participation and generally display values of voluntarism in contrast to the careerism of public service organisations (see Edwards and Hulme, 1992). The actual empirical verification of these comparative advantages in the case of Somalia has yet to be undertaken.

It has also, however, to be recognised that a strength of many NGOs is relief work and that the transition to a rehabilitation and development mode of operations is carried out more selectively. With the closing down of many feeding centres and relief camps in Somalia, significantly a number of NGOs also left. However, whatever social and technical services provided in the field of agricultural extension, education, health and other functions normally associated with public administration, was substantially managed by NGOs, generally with funding from UNOSOM, UNICEF, multilateral and bilateral donors, in addition to their own organisational funding. The Status Report of activities published by the FAO office in Somalia, outlining donor actions in the agricultural sector bears this out. In consequence, there was evidence to suggest that the influence and magnitude of NGO programmes in Somalia exceeded that of any other African crisis in modern times (with the possible exception of Rwanda).

Institutional implications for the transition from emergency to development
The switch from a short to a medium term perspective has implications for NGO activity in terms of institutional coordination and collaboration. Certain NGOs decided to move from an emergency mode of operations to a development mode. An example of this are the NGOs in the Bay Region who programmed 'the establishment of effective village based extension services which will provide a combination of advice and inputs to farmers groups' (Concern/Irish Bilateral Aid Kinsella Report). This suggests that the emergence of NGO-managed district wide extension services, which was similar to conventional agricultural services provision, and employing former government staff.

A major element of the decentralisation of a government function to an NGO is the requirement for public accountability. In the case of research, extension or credit, the accountability proposed is to the Community Councils. This was desirable in terms of public interest and in view of the optimal utilisation of resources as Community Councils could ensure that NGOs are coordinated to avoid duplication and waste. At the grassroots level, NGOs should also work in partnership with the Councils of Elders so that a sustainable institutional base is established.

Conclusions

When the apparatus of the unitary state of Somalia had collapsed, the Somali people, although unified by language, ethnicity and religion, fragmented into clan and sub-clan divisions which became fluid units for political and military action. And as Somali clans are spread in mosaic fashion across the country, political units are unstable and neighbouring alliances between sub-clans may make more strategic sense than affiliations to one's kinsmen in a more remote area, provided the incentives are right.

The resurgence of cultural institutions such as councils of elders and religious fundamentalism to some extent, filled the void left by the demise of the state. The elders became representative spokespersons with both UNOSOM II military and political affairs offices. Claims for kidnappings, compensation and community relations were, in areas outside of Mogadishu, dealt with by the councils of elders. However, the membership of the councils is occasionally problematic as its composition to be effective, should reflect the dominant militia force at a particular historical moment. If certain representatives were politically unpalatable to UNOSOM, hand picked replacements represented little. As observed by Mohamed Abdullahi (1995) UNOSOM 'continued to organize (and pay for) many months of meetings between a plethora of irrelevant and unrepresentative "representatives"'.

The representative character of informal institutions is also critical in terms of the degree to which they advocate the rights of the poor and vulnerable. Dreze and Sen express reservations on the effectiveness of local institutions to reach the poor 'reliance on local institutions to allocate relief is problematic, and can end up being at best indiscriminate and at worst blatantly iniquitous'. To offset this they advocate public action by the citizens through pressure groups and activism. However, it is difficult to apply this model to a stateless society in which political power is diffuse and resource allocation mechanisms as well as entitlements are fluid, erratic and exogenously generated. While advocating the participation of the public in the process of social change; in a state of chaos, without any democratic instruments available to a highly vulnerable population; there can be either extreme powerlessness or possibilities of micro-level self-governance, provided a breakdown of social order does not ensue. Worryingly there was evidence of a breakdown of mutual obligations, family support systems and traditional norms of social welfare in Somalia.

In Somalia, in the vacuum of statelessness, NGOs, including national, international, Islamic and Christian, assumed the role that Church organisations assumed in 16th century Europe; assuming a monopoly of social service provision; education, health and community activism. Ultimately, either by force or negotiation, a political solution will emerge but it is important that NGOs have 'empowered' local communities sufficiently that they can ensure that the distributive mechanisms in a new state can ensure that the powerless and the vulnerable benefit from safety nets and have a real say in the determination of a more stable, brighter future.

References

Abdullahi Mohamed Diriye (1995), 'Fiasco in Somalia: US:UN Intervention', *Occasional Paper*, No. 61, Africa Institute of South Africa, Pretoria.

Dreze, J. and Sen, S. (1989), *Hunger and Public Action*, Clarendon Press, Oxford.

Mullen, J. (1987), 'The Organization and Administration of the Delivery System of Agricultural Services in Somalia with Case Studies', Report prepared for the Ministry of Agriculture and FAO, Rome.

Rondinelli, D.A. (1993), *Development Projects on Policy Experiments*, London.

UNOSOM (1994), *Draft Transitional Charter*, mimeo, UNOSOM, Mogadishu.

4 Rural Poverty Alleviation in China

LIU FENGQIN

Abstract

China's large size and long history has influenced the economic development in rural areas, which are characterized with uneven levels of economic development because of various social, historical and natural reasons. The policy of reform and opening up to the outside world has brought about historical changes in China's rural areas, and the rural people's income and living standards have been greatly improved. However, there are still large numbers of the rural population suffering from a lack of basic needs particularly food and clothing. The Chinese government has attached great importance to poverty alleviation and stressed that the way out of poverty was by reliance on self-management, developing the local economy, using local natural and human resources and applying science and technology. The long-term anti-poverty strategic plan requires that the rural people enhance their self-reliance capability as well as to improve their education and technological levels to meet the challenges. Rural poverty alleviation will not only benefit the poor rural population, but also contribute greatly to the rural economic and social development of the whole of China.

Introduction

China is a large agricultural country with a population of 1.1 billion people, eighty per cent of whom live in rural areas. Therefore, the development of agriculture has a significant impact on the realization of China's modernization because the agricultural sector stands as a pillar in the economy. It is imperative to strengthen the development of agriculture to build China into a modernized and powerful country.

The Chinese government places great emphasis upon the development of agriculture to improve the living standards of its 1.1 billion people. China has only seven per cent of the world's arable land, yet it has to feed twenty-two per cent of the world's population, hence, it is a critical task to develop high-yield, high-quality and high-efficiency agriculture.

China is experiencing the transition from simply meeting farmer's basic needs in food and clothing to developing secure livelihoods. The strengthening of agriculture aims to provide people with abundant agricultural produce and to increase rural households' income from farming, township industries as well as business diversification.

Agricultural development in China

Since 1978, the Chinese government started a new policy of 'reform and opening' to the outside world (*Gaige Kaifang*). China's rural economy has experienced a rapid development since the adoption of the Household Responsibility System (*Jiating Lianchan Chengbao Zeren Zhir*) and the increase in procurement prices for grain which has brought benefits to farmers. According to the Household Responsibility System, the state-owned land is farmed partly by collective and partly by individual households by contract. Each household has managed private plots, usually based proportionately on household size. Other collective assets were sold or contracted to individuals or groups who were willing to manage them. The household was obligated to pay its quota to the state, to make contributions to collective welfare funds, and to contribute labour to maintain the rural public infrastructure. Any produce above the quota can be sold on the free market and all remaining output can be retained by the household. The new system has greatly raised farmer's initiative in agricultural production.

The rural areas have witnessed great historical changes with the development of an ongoing process of reform. The rapid emergence of township enterprises and service industries has brought structural adjustment of rural industry which has created employment opportunities for farmers, especially for rural surplus labourers. Rural people have been encouraged to develop agricultural production and rural economy by applying science and technology, and by exploring local resources. Farmers' income has been increased and their living standards have been improved noticeably.

However, the economic foundation for agriculture is still weak and the rural areas are still fragile in terms of economic capability. Compared with the living standards of most city people, the living conditions and living standards for most farmers still remain at a low level, especially for the farmers living in poverty-stricken areas who will suffer from meeting basic needs of food and clothing.

Rural poverty in China

Uneven levels of economic development persist in China

China's large size and long history has influenced economic development in rural areas. Distinct imbalances of economic development in different regions have occurred because of various social, economic, historical, natural and geographic reasons (see Table 4.1).

Table 4.1 Average per capita net income of the rural people in China (1987)

Income ¥RMB (1$=¥3.71)	Counties (No)	Percentage of the total (%)	Population (million)	Percentage of the total (%)
< 150	53	2.1	14,538	1.7
150 ~ 200	164	6.5	54,385	6.5
200 ~ 300	479	19.0	165,517	19.7
300 ~ 400	532	21.1	188,489	22.4
400 ~ 500	489	19.4	179,818	21.3
500 ~ 700	548	21.7	179,728	21.3
700 ~ 1000	210	8.3	50,951	6.0
> 1000	50	1.9	9,050	1.1

Source: China Agricultural Yearbook, 1988, China Statistics Publishing House, Beijing.

Table 4.1 shows that the rural people's income varies greatly in different regions of China. Rapid economic progress has been achieved in its eastern coastal regions and some other areas, while its western and central regions are relatively poor. It is evident that the gap between the

54

poor regions and the relatively rich regions becomes wider and wider. What is more important is how to bridge the gap which has greatly impacted on the development of China's national economy and social stability.

According to one survey, the poor population numbered 125 million by the end of 1985, taking up 14.8 per cent of the total rural population, and their average per capita income was less than half of the rural people's income in the country. Furthermore, 40 million of the low-income population had a per capita annual income less than 150 yuan RMB and they suffered from a lack of necessary supplies in food, clothing and decent housing. Most of the poor rural people live in remote border areas, ethnic minority areas, deep mountainous areas and the former revolutionary base areas. These areas are generally located in China's central and western regions, covering 664 counties in 22 provinces and regions (Yang Qiulin, 1994, pp. 1-2). According to the state statistics survey, until 1993, there are still 80 million poor population in China, taking up approximately 9 per cent of the country's rural population. Most of these poor areas are now located in the regions with poor natural conditions.

Features of poor areas

Poor areas share some common characteristics, which include mainly:

(a) Low level of productivity growth - primitive production methods, outdated production skills, small-scale markets, simple production structure, poor infrastructure and insufficient supply of food and clothing.

(b) Low level of social development - poor transportation facilities, poor information flow, shortage of technical personnel, poor education and poor medical care.

(c) Poor natural and ecological environment.

(d) Excessive population growth.

Poverty alleviation in China

Policies and measures for 'aiding-the-poor'

The Chinese government attaches great importance to lifting poor farmers out of poverty. Specific surveys have focused on poor areas, while a series of policies and measures to assist the poor have been worked out and conducted in the poor areas. A strategic plan has been designed to solve the problems of poor areas which focuses on the following aspects:

(a) To establish 'aiding-the-poor' organizations at all levels.

(b) To identify the poor areas.

(c) To set up favourable policies and measures, especially offering low-interest loans.

(d) To support the poor areas with necessary investment and materials inputs.

(e) To introduce advanced science and technology.

(f) To establish training plans to improve the rural people's education and technological knowledge.

(g) To create public contributions from the whole society to help the poor areas by establishing cross-linkages.

Two important strategic transitions

Great achievements have been obtained since China started its aiding-the-poor strategic plan in the 1980s. What is most important is that two significant strategic transitions have been realized gradually, i.e.

(a) From dependency to development - and to stress development by self-reliance rather than by relief.

(b) Building a flourishing agriculture by reliance on science and technology, and by improvement of the poor people's education level and technical knowledge.

The Chinese government attaches greater importance to developing the local economy of poor areas rather than to focusing efforts on welfare. More efforts have been made to encourage the poor people to develop pillar industries and a commodity economy by exploring and utilizing the natural resources and the immense human resources. It aims to take advantage of local resources to develop the local economy.

Carrying out poverty-focused projects (*Fupin Xiangmu*) is one of the key aspects to help the poor people. Let's see the following sample.

Hong'an County, located in Hubei province, is a poor county. The director of Hong'an Tea Factory is a farmer enterpriser who studied tea science at Anhui Agricultural College. In 1988 he undertook a tea project and got a low-interest loan from the County. The loan was intended to help the factory develop an old tea plantation, purchase machines and equipment and cooperate with the 14 village tea factories in the area to achieve a combined system of producing and marketing. The director also accepted the task to help the 13 poor households in two nearby villages to improve tea and crop production. Through his one year's hard work, the production output of the factory reached two million RMB, 100,000 kg of high-quality tea was exported abroad and earned foreign exchange in excess of 1.4 million RMB. The 25 farmers in the 13 households earned an annual average income of 1,290 RMB, and the average per capita net income for the 13 households was 422 RMB, which was the highest in the County. Meanwhile the tea factory also helped 120 poor households in another four villages to rise out of poverty. This project is a successful model project in the poor area (Yang Qiulin, 1994, pp. 153-154).

A successful poverty-focused project ultimately helps the poor rural people gradually eliminate poverty and become prosperous.

To help the poor people get rid of poverty, the government has always stressed the importance to further improve the poor people's education level and technical skills. Various training courses have been arranged for poor rural people to facilitate their acquisition of knowledge and skills to fulfil the demanding needs of rural economic development. So far 18,000 rural cadres and specialized technicians and 40 million poor rural people have received successful training according to the national 'Spark Project' (*Xinghuo Jihua*), 'Harvest Project' (*Fengshou Jihua*) and 'Spreading Project' (*Liaoyuan Jihua*). Most of them have learned at least 1-2 technical skills (see Table 4.2). Table 4.2 is based on a sample survey of 500 villages.

Table 4.2 Achievement of 'Spreading Project'

Year	Popularized Technological Skills	Ouput Value (billion) (¥ RMB)	Profit (billion) (¥ RMB)
1988	2,905	2.19	0.84
1989	3,623	2.55	0.71

Source: Zhao Wei, Wang Weimin, 1990.

Conclusions

Anti-poverty programmes in China present a long-term difficult task which, surely, can be accomplished through the poor people's self-management, especially through the adoption of new science and technology. Undoubtedly support from the government is very necessary, however, the investment from the government is limited and it is far from enough to develop the local economy and productivity. Therefore, the poor rural people must build their own confidence, generate local economic strength and what is more important is to enhance their internal vitality and the spirit of self-reliance and self-development which are the key factors contributing to their future prosperity.

The overall economic development in poor areas will benefit millions of people in the poor areas and at the same time accelerate the economic and social development of all China.

References

Qiulin, Yang (1994), *Project Management*, People's Press, Beijing, pp. 1-2.
Qiulin, Yang (1994), *Project Management*, People's Press, Beijing, pp. 153-154.
Wei, Zhao and Weimin, Wang (1990), *A sample Survey Report*.

5 Poverty Reduction Strategies and Programmes in Ghana

KWEKU O A APPIAH

Introduction

Development indicators show that Ghana compares favourably with most other African countries. For example, income distribution is less skewed than in many other sub-Saharan African countries. However, according to the World Bank's classification, Ghana is ranked among the world's low income countries. Moreover, per capita income is lower now than it was in the 1970s and 1960s. The average income (GDP per capita) in Ghana is now equivalent to approximately US$ 450 a year or roughly the same GDP per head as China. These data imply that social conditions in Ghana are poorer than the average for all developing countries. Indeed, even a cursory examination of social conditions in Ghana today show that the quality of life and access to social services such as health care, safe water and sanitation as well as to productive employment and economic services continues to be poor for a large proportion of the population. Furthermore, life expectancy is low; levels of morbidity and infant and child mortality are high and levels of education and literacy are generally unsatisfactory, especially among women.

The bench-mark study on poverty in Ghana is *A Poverty Profile for Ghana 1987-88*, which was based on the first round of the Ghana Living Standards Survey (GLSS 1). This study estimated that in 1988 some 36 per cent of the total population lived in poverty, defined as persons whose mean household expenditures per capita are less than two-thirds of the national average. Almost 10 per cent were estimated to endure hard-core poverty, defined in GLSS 1 as less than one-third of average household expenditure per capita.[1] Additionally, the study found that poverty in Ghana is overwhelmingly a rural phenomenon, with 80 per cent of those persons classified as poor residing in rural areas. Whereas 27 per cent of non-Accra urban residents and 4 per cent of Accra residents that year were classified as being in poverty, 43 per cent of the 67 per cent of Ghanaians who lived in the rural areas were classified as poor.[2] Hard-core poverty is almost entirely confined to rural areas.

The recently published *Ghana Living Standards Survey: Report on the Third Round* (GLSS 3) for the years 1991-92 indicates that there has been some success in poverty reduction. In particular, this survey estimated that the proportion of Ghanaians in poverty had fallen to 31.4 per cent from the 36 per cent recorded by GLSS 1. Surprisingly, however, it was found that urban poverty had risen since 1988. For example, the incidence of poverty in Accra accounted for 6 per cent of overall poverty compared to 4 per cent in 1988. As these data show, the rate of improvement in poverty reduction is low and poverty remains severe. The stark reality is that at current rates of economic growth and population increase of about 5 and 3 per cent per annum, respectively, the average poor person would not cross over the poverty line for another half a century.

This paper outlines poverty in Ghana, in terms of the household characteristics of the poor; reviews some of the major policies and programmes for poverty alleviation and reduction; and summarises some of the lessons that have been learned. The paper begins, however, with a chronology of events that gave rise to the policy focus on poverty.

Background to contemporary poverty programmes in Ghana

The decade of the 1980s, which witnessed dramatic reversals in economic and social development in sub-Saharan Africa and other regions of the world is now part of historical record. In Ghana, the steep economic decline which dominated the period up to 1983, actually commenced as early as the mid-1960s with more rapid deterioration setting in from about 1975. Inflation, below 10 per cent in 1970, rose to nearly 30 per cent in 1975 and exceeded 100 per cent in 1983. Government revenue dropped from over 16 per cent of GDP in 1975 to 7 per cent in 1983. Public sector investment plunged from around 6 per cent of GDP in the mid-1970s to less than 1 per cent in 1983, resulting in severe deterioration in the nation's economic and social infrastructure. Between 1975 and 1983 real GDP dropped by over 10 per cent and real income per capita by 27 per cent. Thus by the early 1980s, the Ghanaian economy was in a critical condition.

Worse still, the cumulative effect of continued and increasing over-valuation of the cedi eroded all incentives to produce for export or to market through formal channels. Imports significantly reduced as foreign currency reserves became exhausted. Drastic and chronic shortages, if not total absence, of imported intermediate and consumer goods reduced the productive capacity of local industries and also created serious hardships for the population, particularly the poor and less affluent.

The effect on social services was pronounced. Per capita expenditure in real terms on health fell from 6.36 per cent in 1974 to 0.65 per cent in 1982/83. By 1984 around 50 per cent of medical practitioners had left the country. With shortages of drugs, materials and personnel hospital attendance dropped substantially. For example, attendance fell by about 41 per cent and 67 per cent in the capital, Accra, and another large town (Cape Coast), respectively. The maternal mortality rate was 5-15/1,000 and the crude death rate 19-20/1,000. Poverty related diseases became widespread and included diseases, previously eliminated, which had resurfaced. Food supplies became limited; per capita food availability in 1983 was 30 per cent lower than in 1974. The food price indices for locally produced food in 1970, 1980 and 1983, were 10.5, 392.5 and 2,754.6, respectively.

It was within these desperate social and economic circumstances that the government of the Provisional National Defence Council (PNDC), which had come into power on December 31st, 1981, took the decision to formulate and implement policies to stem and then reverse the decline. These policies were articulated within the framework of the Economic Recovery Programme (ERP) which encompassed a series of Structural Adjustment Programmes (SAPs). The aim of the first phase of the ERP (1983-86) was to stabilise the economy. This was to be achieved through the correction of internal and external imbalances. Principal objectives included:

(i) elimination of the over-valuation of the currency
(ii) reduction in the budget deficit
(iii) establishment of tight control over money supply and bank credit
(iv) to begin rehabilitation of essential economic and social
infrastructure.

The second phase of the ERP (1986-89) focused primarily on the restoration of sustained growth. Consequently, in pursuit of enhanced economic performance, this phase sought the achievement of significant reforms in the following:

(i) incentives to producers of exports
(ii) ownership and management of parastatals

61

(iii) the civil service
(iv) the financial system
(v) the educational system.

In economic terms, the initial results of the SAPs were very impressive. The budget deficit was reduced from 90 per cent to 30 per cent of government revenue in 1983 and was in balance in the following year, with positive real GDP growth restored. Furthermore, continued fiscal discipline yielded increased budgetary ˙ surpluses thereby enabling government to reduce its indebtedness to the banking system and increase its contribution to public sector investment. Thus the Structural Adjustment Programmes achieved considerable success in stabilising the economy.

However this stabilisation did not, nor was it designed to, redress some of the fundamental structural deficiencies of the economy and the social problems which these induced. Indeed, the adverse social consequences of Ghana's prolonged economic decline, which had been particularly severe in the case of the poor and other vulnerable groups, were actually exacerbated by some of the policy measures of the SAPs such as devaluation, liberalisation of prices and redeployment. Thus despite the immediate positive impact of the ERP, as reflected by key economic indicators, it became evident quite early into the programme, that overall improvements in the lives of the vast majority of ordinary people would take longer to materialise.[3]

The deprivation suffered by the vulnerable was compellingly outlined in a UNICEF study published in 1986.[4] This study revealed a picture of unremitting deterioration in key social indicators arising from increasing poverty, inadequate nutrition and ineffective social services between the late 1970s and early 1980s. To illustrate, the study estimated that the proportion of the population below an absolute poverty line determined by UNICEF rose from 60-65 per cent to 65-75 per cent in rural areas between the late 1970s and early 1980s. In urban areas, the increase was from 30-35 per cent to 45-50 per cent. Another finding was that average calorie availability as a percentage of requirements fell from 97 per cent in 1970 to 88 per cent in the late 1970s and then to only 68 per cent in the early 1980s. It was also estimated that the infant mortality rate rose from 86 per 1,000 live births in the late 1970s to 107-120 per 1,000 live births in the early 1980s.

The study also showed that the negative social impact of the SAPs was significantly worse for people who lived in those parts of the country that had historically been substantially below the national average for social indicators. These areas which are characterized by structural and endemic poverty, difficult environmental conditions and poor social infrastructure and services are mainly in the northern regions which fall within Ghana's savannah zone. Therefore, while there were pre-existing conditions which gave rise to the disparities between the northern regions and the more southernly regions it was evident that the SAPs, initially at least, worsened rather than improved matters.[5]

UNICEF's documentation of Ghana's social crisis coincided with a number of significant domestic and global developments. Domestically, Ghanaian policy-makers, having successfully tackled the immediate economic tasks of stabilisation and restoration of growth, began to become increasingly sensitive to the social dimensions of adjustment. As a consequence and also in response to the problems that had been identified by the UNICEF study, a process was initiated in July 1986 that culminated in the birth in November 1987 of the Programme of Actions to Mitigate the Social Costs of Adjustment (PAMSCAD).[6]

On the global front, serious and vigorous debate had begun on the content, realism and impact of orthodox stabilisation and adjustment programmes. The issues were forcefully placed on the agenda by the publication in 1987 of UNICEF's *Adjustment with a Human Face* and further developed by the United Nations Economic Commission For Africa's International Conference on the Human Dimensions of Africa's Economic Recovery held in Khartoum, Sudan in 1988. Thus, by the end of the 1980s there was a general acknowledgement and concern about the persistence of the negative social impact of economic adjustment programmes throughout Africa as well as in developing countries in other regions.

The global critique of adjustment programmes stressed the following major points:

(i)   structural impediments to the effective operation of markets necessitated a long time horizon for economic and social reform;

(ii) reforms in policies and programmes, though necessary, could also aggravate the condition of the poor and vulnerable and, thus, reverse past gains as well as undermine social and political stability; and

(iii) that stabilisation and adjustment programmes could be designed from the start to have a "human face", that is, reflect much greater sensitivity towards poverty issues in general and social development in particular.

PAMSCAD

PAMSCAD was introduced, as its title implies, to ameliorate some of the immediate adverse effects of economic stabilisation and adjustment. Contrary to contemporaneous calls for a fundamental re-design of adjustment programmes, PAMSCAD did no more than to graft on to the ongoing SAP a number of interventions to 'mitigate' the negative social side effects or costs of the economic development programmes.[7] The design of PAMSCAD was guided by three major policy considerations. These were[8]:

(i) to address present and likely short-term conditions of poverty and deprivation of the poor groups, either stemming from pre-existing poverty or measures in the design of the adjustment programme;

(ii) to use the success of stabilisation and adjustment measures to more effectively allocate resources to meet needs of the poor in a consistent and systematic manner; and

(iii) to enhance the sustainability and acceptability of the ERP.

In operational terms, PAMSCAD consisted of 23 projects that were undertaken in five broad areas of intervention, namely, community initiative, employment generation, assistance for the redeployed, basic needs and education. The programme areas were identified on the basis of the characteristics as well as source of vulnerability of target groups. In addition, projects selected for implementation were required to possess the following characteristics[9]:

(i) a strong poverty focus;

(ii) a high economic and social rate of return and where quantification was not feasible, a strong poverty focus, cost-effectiveness, deepening of the social dimensions of adjustment, avoidance of distortions and possible economic value even though unquantifiable;

(iii) ease and speed of implementation, without necessitating the creation of new institutional arrangements;

(iv) avoidance of any future obligations for recurrent costs;

(v) consistency with the approach and objectives of the ERP; and

(f) political marketability and currency.

With regard to institutional arrangements, PAMSCAD relied almost exclusively on government ministries and agencies. In addition, the ministries of Finance and Economic Planning and Local Government were assigned joint responsibility for integrating PAMSCAD with the adjustment programme. Only one project, food-for-work, was assigned for implementation to a non-governmental organization (NGO). The projects were spread across nine different ministerial sectors, namely, local government, mobilisation and social welfare, roads and highways, industry, agriculture, lands and mineral resources, water and sanitation, health and education.

The total cost of the programme was estimated at US$ 83.9 million of which the foreign exchange component was US$ 37.6 million. More than a third of the projects and 42 per cent of the total budgetary allocation was accounted for by employment generation with the remaining projects distributed, in descending order of importance, to redeployment, basic needs, community initiative and education.

As for grass-roots participation, it was hoped that the community initiative projects (CIPs) would help to rekindle the spirit of self-help in Ghanaian communities and encourage their participation in development activities jointly with government. The major incentive for community participation was the availability of matching funds from Government, which covered varying proportions of the cost of micro-projects focused principally on the social sectors. The residual after government funding (which was usually considerably larger than the matching fund) was meant to be funded by community contributions and support from the District Assembly, whether in cash or kind.

Evaluation of PAMSCAD

The experience with PAMSCAD provided a number of important lessons about the design and management of poverty alleviation programmes as well as the conceptualisation of poverty as a phenomenon.[10] The main conclusion which emerged from the various evaluations of PAMSCAD is that it was not an appropriate instrument for sustainable poverty alleviation, a judgement that the Government arrived at about midway through the programme.

Key observations of evaluations included the following:

(i)   the conceptualisation of the programme reflected an inadvertent but nonetheless entrenched contemporary tendency to marginalise issues of poverty and vulnerability from mainstream development policy and planning. This arose from a perception of poverty alleviation and reduction as a charitable event which contributed to the compartmentalisation of poverty concerns outside macro and sectoral policies and programmes;

(ii) the ameliorative focus of the programme gave rise to an inadequate consideration of the causes of poverty relative to the effects. As a consequence, the benefits of the programme were liable to being both limited and unsustainable;

(iii) the programme was defective both in design and management and unsuited for sustainable poverty reduction. Some of the deficiencies included insufficient involvement of target groups in planning, implementation and monitoring; a neglect of institution-building at the grass-roots involving the poor and vulnerable; and a tendency towards centralisation of key programme management responsibilities within national ministries or agencies.

Despite these criticisms, PAMSCAD clearly served a useful ameliorative purpose with regard to providing some short-term relief to some poor and vulnerable population groups. However, in response to the recognised need for a more satisfactory and sustainable approach to poverty reduction than PAMSCAD, and inspired by UNDP's Human Development Report, the Government decided to formulate a comprehensive human development strategy for Ghana. Accordingly, a conceptual and policy framework for addressing the challenges of human development and poverty reduction was developed.[11] This has informed all subsequent policy work by the NDPC, including *Ghana - Vision 2020: The First Step* (which is a co-ordinated programme of economic and social development policies for the five years, 1996-2000 that the President presented to Parliament in January, 1995).

Characteristics of the poor

There is as yet no consensus on, let alone an officially sanctioned, poverty line in Ghana. The measure that has gained currency is that adopted by the World Bank and the Ghana Statistical Service. His measure is based upon real household total expenditure, expressed in per capita terms. Selection of this measure is, in part, determined by the greater accuracy and reliability of household expenditures than household income as a measure of the economic welfare of individuals and households.

Two poverty lines, an upper and lower, have been set for purposes of assessing the levels of deprivation, for example in terms of caloric intake, implied for individuals unable to achieve these expenditure levels. The upper line is pegged at two-thirds mean household expenditures per capita, while the lower line is fixed at one-half of mean household expenditures per capita. Although arbitrarily determined, these lines are used to classify the poor and 'hard core' or very poor, respectively.

For purposes of policy analysis and prescription on poverty, two poverty indices are used. One, the 'head-count' ratio measures the fraction of poor units in the population and indicates the incidence of poverty. The second, the poverty gap index, reflects both the incidence and depth of poverty and provides a measure of the income that is required to eradicate poverty under perfect targeting.

In terms of economic characteristics the poor are involved in a variety of sectors and occupations. Overall, poverty is concentrated among two major socio-economic groups: food-crop farmers and self-employed workers, who together accounted for 77 per cent of total poverty (based on head-count and poverty-gap ratios) in 1992. Nearly three-quarters of the economically active members of poor households are self-employed, of whom about 80 per cent are in agriculture (mostly as food-crop farmers). Besides this the poor are also to be found working in small-scale enterprises and micro-enterprises in the urban formal and informal sectors in occupations that range from trade, crafts and services; about nine per cent were public sector employees. Sources of income typically include crops and livestock, forestry and fisheries, participation to the labour market, self-employment in micro-enterprises, and migration and remittances. Both the incidence and depth of poverty among food-crop farmers and self-employed workers fell between 1988 and 1992. Except for public sector employees, significant reductions in poverty were also experienced during this period by other groups such as export crop farmers and private informal sector employees.

Testimony on the gender dimension of poverty in Ghana is provided by the findings of the GLSS surveys that show that the lowest standards of living are suffered by rural females. The link between gender (in terms of the sex of the head of household) and poverty is not clear, however. Even so, widows, aged women or those without adult children are more likely to be poor, especially in the rural north. Women's poverty is exacerbated and deepened by bias against women in access to land, credit and education; resources are still primarily directed towards men. This is notwithstanding the predominance of women in agriculture and rural non-farm activities and an increasing dependence of households on women's earnings. Women in Ghana, particularly those in rural areas, are therefore largely discriminated against and remain deprived in their efforts to improve their social status, conditions and circumstances.

In terms of demographic characteristics, there is a positive correlation between household size and poverty in Ghana. On average the poor, especially the very poor, have much larger household sizes (a mean of 6.3 members in 1992) than the non-poor (a mean of 3.6 members). This finding is underscored by the fact that the larger households are disproportionately represented in the Rural Savannah, which is by far the poorest area in the country. By contrast, Accra, where households are smallest on average, is the locality least affected by poverty.

The correlation between household size and poverty can be attributed, at least in part, to the age composition and economic status of household members as these characteristics determine the consumption and productivity levels of households. Households with high age dependency ratios[12] are likely to be less productive than those that have more members in the economically active age group, all other things being equal. According to the GLSS studies, around 60 per cent of poor household members are either below the age of 15 or above 65. Among the non-poor, the ratio is 44 per cent.

Levels of education and literacy and numeracy rates are significantly lower among the poor than amongst the non-poor. According to GLSS 2 (1989) only 38 per cent of the poor could read whereas about 61 per cent of the non-poor could. The low level of educational achievement among the poor is particularly significant given that education is an important determinant of productivity owing to its role in skills acquisition. Productivity is, in turn, an important determinant of household welfare.

In terms of health, the overall health status of Ghanaians is currently unsatisfactory as manifested by the low average life expectancy and high rates of infant and child mortality. Much of this is attributable to endemic, put preventable, diseases. Although these diseases (mainly malaria, acute respiratory infections and water-borne diseases) are prevalent throughout the country their incidence is proportionately greater among people who live in the midst of poor environmental conditions and low standards of personal hygiene; in short, the poor.

Available evidence indicates that the current nutrition situation in Ghana, especially among young children and pregnant women, is also far from satisfactory. Infants and children in rural areas are especially disadvantaged and vulnerable. Malnutrition is found everywhere in the country. However, its incidence and manifestations are generally more serious in rural areas, especially in the North, Upper East, Upper West, Central and Western regions. It is as serious in some urban and fishing communities in the southern coastal plains area.

The GLSS studies confirm that poverty in Ghana is overwhelmingly a rural phenomenon. About 80 per cent of the nation's poor and almost all of those classified as the hard-core poor are in rural areas.[13] The incidence of poverty is highest in the Savannah, Volta basin and Mid-coast zones, with hard-core poverty being most pronounced in the Savannah and Mid-coast areas, as well as in parts of the Mid-forest zone. There are also significant regional variations in the incidence of poverty, especially between northern and southern Ghana.

The experience of poverty in Ghana

As may be expected, the GLSS studies confirm that the poor have less access to social services, particularly education and health services, than the non-poor. As a result, levels of education and literacy and numeracy rates are significantly lower among the poor than amongst the non-poor as are school attendance rates across various age groups. According to GLSS 2 (1989) only 38 per cent of the poor could read whereas about 61 per cent of the non-poor could. in terms of enrolment even though the proportion of the population aged 6 and above that ever attended school increased from 61 per cent to 66 per cent between 1988-92, large variations exist among income groups and among regions. Children in Accra and other urban areas were more inclined to attend school than children living in rural areas who are generally the poor, especially children in rural savannah. For example, the net enrolment rate for girls aged 6 and 11 from very poor families in rural savannah was only 33 per cent in 1988 increasing to 36 per cent in 1992. The rate for girls from very poor families in Accra was 60 per cent in 1988 and increased to 86 per cent in 1992. Secondary school enrolment also declines with increased poverty.

As far as access to health services is concerned, the GLSS studies found that higher proportions of the non-poor than the very poor consult medical personnel when ill. It was also found that urban residents consult medical personnel more than rural residents with the figure ranging from a low of 36.1 per cent to a high of 59.2 per cent in Accra in 1987/88. An explanatory factor for this finding is the substantially lower average income of the rural population compared to those of urban residents. Another explanatory factor is the skewed distribution of social infrastructure in favour of urban areas such that people in urban areas have on average considerably easier physical access to health facilities than those in rural areas. Another difference found between socio-economic groups is the type of medical personnel consulted during illness. Thus people in the higher income brackets have a higher propensity to consult formally trained medical personnel when ill than those in the lower expenditure levels. On the other hand, the poor, especially those in rural areas, tend to consult herbalists and traditional healers.

One of the most serious social problems which contributes to the magnitude of poverty in Ghana is the acute shortage of opportunities for stable, gainful employment. Not only is this a problem in the present but over the long-term the increasingly youthful structure of Ghana's population as well as the rate of population growth give rise to serious cause for concern about the capacity of the labour market to provide productive employment to the country's labour force. The employment problem currently manifests itself in the form of both open unemployment and underemployment. In rural areas the major problem is underemployment. This is clearly a major contributor to the high incidence of rural poverty. Underemployment is also found in urban areas among those active in the informal sector. There is also a high level of unemployment in urban areas.

Even though most people of working age are engaged in some form of economic activity, mostly farming, they are unable to use their abilities to the full and their productivity and earnings are low. GLSS 1 found that over half - 55.6 per cent - of the incomes of all Ghanaians was derived from agriculture, followed by income from other forms of self-employment which contributes 28.2 per cent. Income from employment provided only 7.3 per cent of household incomes. For the poor, the comparable figures were 65.1 per cent from agriculture, 22.8 per cent from other forms of self-employment and only 4.4 per cent from employment.

Food is a major item of expenditure for all Ghanaians and its share in total household expenditure has increased as a result of inflationary pressures coupled with sluggish growth in real incomes. For example, GLSS 1 recorded cash expenditure on food accounting for 42.6 per cent of total expenditure. Total expenditure on food averaged 66.6 per cent, of which just over one-third is the estimated value of food produced and consumed by the household. Outlay on food by the poor is only slightly higher at 69.1 per cent of total expenditure, but their consumption of home-produced food is much higher at 33 per cent of total expenditure or nearly half the value of food consumption. Comparable figures for the hard-core poor are 70.7 per cent and 32.2 per cent.

Water is essential to human life and the search for good quality water supplies has been a fundamental part of human existence since time immemorial. This problem is far from being overcome in many Ghanaian communities and most especially in the rural areas, where the bulk of Ghana's poor reside. While about 93 per cent of urban dwellers are estimated to have access to safe water, only 39 per cent of the rural population have similar access. Consequently, most rural communities rely on ponds and streams as their source of water, resulting in undue exposure to guinea-worm, bilharzia and other water-borne diseases in rural areas. Such conditions exacerbate the health problems of the poor and contributes to their reduced life expectancy. Although considerably better than rural water supply, urban water supply is generally less than satisfactory, especially in slum and other high population density areas where water supply infrastructure has been overstretched.

A related problem is sanitation. Present systems and practices for the safe disposal of solid and liquid waste in both urban and rural areas are inadequate. While sanitation services are unquestionably inadequate, a major contributory factor to sanitation problems is people's behaviour. Members of the public, especially the poor and uneducated, are generally unaware of the potential hazard to health and of the resultant environmental degradation caused by their behaviour and habits. For example, health hazards are created by urban drains which are often choked full of refuse and stagnant water. Sanitation problems are frequently most deplorable in peri-urban slum areas. This is largely due to the fact that a high proportion of rural migrants to the towns and cities settle in these areas, thereby creating a unique set of health and social problems.

Poverty reduction and current governmental policies and strategies

Ghana is committed to the achievement to poverty reduction. This is reflected in the overall long term aim of national development policy to establish Ghana as a middle-income country with a commensurate quality of life and standard of living for the average Ghanaian by the year 2020. In terms of social policy, the over-arching goals for national development as stated in *Ghana Vision 2020: The First Step, 1996-2000* include:

- long, healthy and productive life for the individual with access to an enlarged range of choices for employment, shelter and leisure activities;

- elimination of the extremes of deprivation, reduction of poverty and achievement and maintenance of minimum material conditions for all;

- strengthened and improved human capabilities;

- increased and equitable opportunities for acquisition of knowledge as well as access to the resources necessary for income generation;

- equitable enjoyment of the benefits of national output.

Government and World Bank reports show that poverty declined in Ghana between 1988 and 1992 in all areas except Accra. The declines were most pronounced in rural areas especially in the poorest area, the Rural Savannah, where the head-count ratio fell from 49 per cent in 1988 to 38 per cent in 1992. On the other hand, in Accra, poverty was estimated to have increased from 9 per cent in 1988 to 23 per cent in 1992. Interestingly, while improvements in economic welfare is believed to have benefited the lowest income groups most, the evidence in Accra suggests that the increased poverty in the city resulted from a disproportionately adverse impact of macroeconomic reforms on middle income groups (mostly public sector employees) relative to poorer socio-economic groups.

These developments notwithstanding, the fact remains that over 30 per cent of Ghana's population was below the poverty line in 1992. Moreover, since 1992 there have been clear signs of faltering in social and economic progress, implying reversals in poverty reduction.[14] This is attributable to a slow down in economic growth arising, at least in part, from macroeconomic instability induced by inadequate fiscal and monetary discipline in recent years. Left uncorrected, the deceleration in economic growth will constrain efforts to reduce poverty.

The characteristics, spread and incidence of poverty in Ghana, as sketched above, define the broad areas in which policy actions are required for poverty reduction. These issues are effectively addressed in the strategy for human development proposed by the NDPC in 1991. The strategy has three major elements. The first part is primarily directed toward poverty *alleviation* and putting a halt to further deterioration in levels of deprivation. The second part of the strategy focuses on poverty *reduction*; while the third part consists of programmes to underpin, consolidate, maintain and continuously enhance the social and economic development of the nation. Each phase of the strategy has different commencement and target dates for completion and is designed to overlap with the others. Execution of the strategy is to be tracked by a surveillance system that monitors and analyses progress in poverty reduction as well as identifying new causes of poverty.

The immediate goal of the first phase is to halt and prevent deterioration of the material conditions in which the poor and disadvantaged live and improve their chances for leading longer, healthier, more productive and more satisfying lives. The first phase should not exceed five to seven years and should therefore be completed by about the year 2000 or shortly thereafter. Substantial progress in achieving its objectives will make it possible to begin to concentrate more resources on the next part of the strategy. Priority objectives within this phase include:

(i) from a social perspective, the eradication of malnutrition, establishment of household food security, reduction of infant and maternal mortality, improvement of health and education status and access to social services, reduction of the population growth rate, improvement in the circumstances of women and children;

(ii) from an economic perspective, the reduction and control of inflation, significant increase in employment opportunities, reduction of underemployment, increased productivity and improved access to credit, economic services and markets; and, finally

(iii) from a spatial perspective, initiation of interventions to reduce the marked regional and rural-urban disparities and variations that currently exist.

The second part of the strategy, parts of which are included in the first phase, encompasses programmes to enhance the capacity of the poor to provide for themselves; to increase their incomes; and to improve their quality of life, requires long-term actions which will probably run well into the first decade of the next millennium.

The third part of the strategy consists of programmes to underpin, consolidate, maintain and continuously enhance the social and economic development of the nation. These cover those activities which will ensure qualitative improvements in human capital formation, further improvements and upgrading of the public administration systems at central and local levels and the provision of economic and social infrastructure on a nationwide basis. As with the other phases, there are related programmes currently under way to achieve these objectives. However, it is clear from the developmental nature of these activities that this part will require very long-term effort.

In addition to programmes that enhance the productive capabilities of the poor, reduction of poverty at the individual and household levels requires an environment that not only enables but also empowers the poor, especially women. In other words, the main thrust of the strategy is on helping people to help themselves. This will be complemented by policies and programmes to promote the generation of additional employment and incomes. Employment and income-generation will be pursued in rural areas primarily through the development of agriculture and agro-based industries. Particular attention will necessarily be paid to small-holders and small-scale enterprises. In urban areas, training and job placement schemes will be provided to assist unemployed young men and women to find productive work.

With about two-thirds of the population and the majority of the poor residing in the rural areas, the question of poverty reduction and even national development in Ghana is essentially synonymous with the challenges of rural development. A corollary of this is that the agricultural sector and its development will be pivotal in poverty reduction as it provides sustenance and employment to the rural poor. Moreover, a significant proportion of manufacturing and services industries is devoted to the processing of agricultural commodities and agriculture is the primary source of food supplies for the population. The long-term development of agriculture, especially increasing productivity in the sector, is thus essential to the maintenance of food security, employment generation and poverty reduction.

Some lessons from Ghana's experience

The lessons that have been learned in Ghana as a result of the various initiatives and interventions to alleviate or reduce poverty in the country largely echo and confirm current thinking on poverty reduction strategies. Among the main messages are the following:

(i) A matter pertinent to achievement of poverty reduction that was recognised almost a decade ago is the need for a long-term, sustainable process and strategy However, notwithstanding this awareness and the enunciation of a credible comprehensive, coherent and cohesive strategy for poverty reduction as articulated by the NDPC in 1991, Ghana has yet to begin to effectively address poverty reduction in a systematic and coordinated fashion.   Ironically, Government established a poverty coordinating committee in July 1995 to develop 'a meaningful and effective poverty-reducing strategy ... [and] ... establish the policy agenda on poverty for the coming years' (World Bank, 1995).[15] The intermittent nature of these initiatives, coupled with their inconclusive outcomes to date, is symptomatic of at least two fundamental problems. The first is an adequate understanding of the nature and causes of poverty among key policy makers. The second and possibly more important problem, is the limited political will to stay the course on long-term complex programmes for poverty reduction.[16] Hence a *sine qua non* for the implementation of poverty reduction strategies is the existence of strong, focused and committed leadership to drive and guide the process.

These problems and their seriousness notwithstanding, the capacity to substantially and rapidly reduce poverty largely exists in Ghana, provided that government will establish a clear mandate and an enabling environment to do so. In this regard, and as a first step, there is a strong need for government and the other political parties to go beyond rhetoric to demonstrate clear, unambiguous and concrete commitment to poverty reduction. A possible way out of this quandary is to involve parliaments or other legislative bodies as well as civil society. In this respect, a catalytic role may be played by advocacy groups. Parliamentarians have an important and vital role to play in ensuring the success of poverty reduction programmes. By explicitly embracing poverty reduction as a priority matter, Parliaments can sustain the nation's sensitivity to the needs of the poor in society and ensure commitment to poverty reduction. Another crucial contribution

75

of parliamentarians is to ensure adequate financial provision is made for poverty related programmes in proposed public expenditure.

Pertinent to this issue is the need to strengthen community involvement and participation as integral elements in decision making and in the development process. This involves systems of governance and administration, particularly decentralisation.

(ii) Another vital message from Ghana's experience is the importance of maintaining macroeconomic stability and keeping inflation low. As has been pointed out, despite the many creditable achievements of the Economic Recovery Programme and structural adjustment in Ghana, there has been a persistent failure to effectively curtail inflation. High rates of inflation such as those currently being experienced in Ghana, erode real incomes and standards of living for the poor and rich alike with adverse consequences for their welfare.[17] Moreover, because the country's poor spend about 70 per cent of their income on food, the trend in inflation has serious implications for the welfare and nutritional status of children and women in poor households. There is therefore a compelling need to establish and maintain fiscal and monetary policies that do not fuel inflation.

(iii) Yet another message, relating to the issue of political will, concerns the incidence of public spending. An essential requirement in any poverty reduction strategy is to ensure that public expenditures intended for the poor are actually allocated to projects or services used by them rather than other groups. However, reviews of public expenditure in Ghana consistently show that the poor frequently receive a disproportionately lower share of public expenditures than other socio-economic groups. This no doubt results from the fact that they typically constitute the weakest and politically least empowered groups in society. Hence strong political commitment and will to safeguard and promote the interests of the poor is required for the successful reduction of poverty. This is especially so in circumstances in which resources are very limited and for which competition is intense.

(iv) Of particular significance for sustained poverty reduction is the need for policies and strategies that emphasize helping people to help themselves. The poor, especially women and other vulnerable groups, regardless of whether they are rural or urban dwellers, employ wide ranging measures to sustain themselves. However, where government and donor agencies have acted to assist the poor, their interventions

76

have frequently tended to ignore the traditional coping mechanisms of the poor instead of building on them and incorporating them into a comprehensive matrix of mutually supportive activities. As a result many of these interventions have ended in failure because they have not been appropriately adapted to the circumstances of the intended beneficiaries.

Happily, there are signs that appropriate measures to incorporate traditional mechanisms in the design of poverty reduction programmes are at least being considered in Ghana. For example, within the financial sector initiatives are under way to expand and improve upon non-formal methods of saving.

A related issue concerns the need to re-orientate bureaucratic perceptions, prejudices and, where necessary, practices. To illustrate, there is considerable room for improvement in the reform of urban bye-laws that have a negative impact on informal sector activities. Hence the periodic but nonetheless continuing efforts of the authorities in Ghana's major cities to drive hawkers, pedlars, food sellers and other poor or underemployed people off urban streets. Options such as establishing appropriately regulated pedestrian malls should be explored as a means for achieving a sustainable, pro-poor and people-friendly solution to some of our urban problems.

(v) Finally, it is evident that in order to successfully implement and sustain poverty reduction strategies better use of the civil service and other public institutions is required. Toward this end the public services must be reformed, strengthened and provided with incentives to perform effectively.

Notes

1. The lower poverty line was subsequently changed to one-half of mean household expenditures per capita in GLSS 3; see pp. 7-8.
2. Accra is the capital and largest city in Ghana with a population currently estimated to compromise around 15 per cent of the national total.
3. It should be noted that some groups, mostly the urban elites and those engaged in distribution, extractive sectors and business services, made immediate and substantial gains as a result of the ERP.
4. Adjustment Policies and Programmes to Protect Children and other Vulnerable Groups. (Accra: UNICEF-Ghana, 1986) cited in Saleh, 1993.

5. Since the launch of the ERP and implementation of the SAP, data have shown some modest improvements in health, nutritional and educational status. Thus, these programmes did at least prevent worsening in the quality of life in the longer run.
6. See Government of Ghana, Programme of Actions to Mitigate the Social Costs of Adjustment. (Accra: November, 1987).
7. There was, however, clear recognition at the time of the need to establish means for linking '.... the short-term horizon of PAMSCAD with a long-term, sustainable process and strategy for broad-based socio-economic development' (GOG, 1987).
8. See GOG, 1987.
9. Ibid.
10. See World Bank et al 'Report of the Donor Review Mission on PAMSCAD', Accra, August.
11. These were articulated in a report prepared by the NDPC in 1991 entitled, *Making People Matter*.
12. Defined as the proportion of household members who fall within the under 15 and over 64 years age groups to those of working age, i.e. 15-64 years.
13. However, the incidence of poverty rose in urban areas, particularly Accra, between 1988 and 1992.
14. There have been no poverty assessments since 1992. However, work on a new poverty survey was initiated in August this year.
15. A similar body, the Social Sector Task Force, was set up in 1987 to guide the design and oversee implementation of PAMSCAD.
16. Given the prevalence of unforeseen crises that can be induced by economic shocks, natural disasters or other calamities, it is only to be expected that the best laid plans and programmes can occasionally be knocked off course.
17. This is especially true for the urban poor.

References

Appiah, Kweku O.A. (1995), 'National Planning for Poverty Reduction: Current Social, Economic and Spatial Policy Concerns', paper presented at Seminar on Broad-Based Planning for Poverty Reduction with Democratic Institutions, Accra, November.

Appiah, Kweku O.A. (1995), 'Poverty in Ghana', paper presented at Workshop on Planning and Poverty Reduction in a Transitional Economy, Accra, July.

Boateng, E.O., Ewusi, K., Kanbur, R. and McKay, A. (1990), 'A Poverty Profile for Ghana 1987-88', Social Dimensions of Adjustment in Sub-Sahara Africa *Working Paper 5*, The World Bank, Washington D.C.

Cornia, G.A. et al (1987), *Adjustment With a Human Face*, Vols. I and II, Oxford, Oxford University Press.

Ghana Statistical Service (1995), 'Ghana Living Standards Survey: Report on the Third Round', (GLSS 3), Accra, March.

Government of Ghana (1995), *Ghana - Vision 2020 (The First Step: 1996-2000)*, Presidential Report to Parliament on Co-ordinated programme of Economic and Social Development Policies (Policies for the Preparation of the 1996-2000 Developmental Plan), Assembly Press, January.

Government of Ghana (1987), *Programme of Actions to Mitigate the Social Costs of Adjustment*, Accra, November.

National Development Planning Commission (1991), 'Making People Matter: A Human Development Strategy for Ghana', (mimeo) December.

Norton, Andy, David Korboe, Ellen Bortei-Doku and D.K. Tony Dogbe (1995), 'Poverty Assessment in Ghana using Qualitative and Participatory Research Methods', World Bank, Washington D.C., (mimeo), April.

Saleh, Turhan (1993), 'Designing and Managing Poverty Alleviation Programmes: The PAMSCAD Experience and its Lessons', paper presented at National Seminar on Strengthening Capacity for Planning and Maintaining Poverty Alleviation Policies and Programmes in Ghana, Accra, May.

World Bank (1995), 'Ghana: Poverty Past, Present and Future', West Central Africa Department, Report No. 14504-GH, Washington D.C., June.

World Bank et al (1990), 'Report of the Donor Review Mission on PAMSCAD', Accra, August.

6 Empowering Local Communities: Comilla Approach and Experiences

SALEHUDDIN AHMED[1]

Introduction: rural people, rural areas

Development is a set of conscious efforts directed toward economic, social and political change that takes place in a community or a society as it evolves from a traditional state. The transformation to modern status includes social and political consciousness, division of labour, literacy, urbanization, industrialization and a broad general *participation* in the overall development activities at national, regional, local and village level. UNESCO defines the goals, objectives and the aims of development to be: 'not to develop things but to develop people'. The implication of this approach is that 'development must be aimed at spiritual, moral and material advancement of the whole human being, both as a member of society and from the point of view of individual fulfilment' (Poostchi, 1986).

Rural development has often been defined as having as its main objective the overall balanced and proportionate well-being of rural people. How it works, and the approach it takes, is determined and influenced by many factors in the rural areas of the country. Factors such as the stage of economic development of the country; the attitude of its people; the sincerity, wisdom, skill of its planners, administrators and implementors at all levels; the relevant institutions; the extent to which its citizens are informed, consulted and encouraged to participate; and other factors at the local, village, area, regional and national levels, all affect its direction, its magnitude, its success and failure.

Another definition of rural development (Webster, 1975) considers it as a process which leads to a rise in the capacity of rural people to control their environment resulting from more extensive use of the benefits which is ensured from such a control. Although this definition falls short on some of the objectives of rural development, increased benefits could be reflected in all or some of the following indicators of rural development:

(a) Change in agricultural productivity, reflected in per hectare yield.

(b) Changes in the rate of employment, unemployment and underemployment.

(c) Changes in the distribution of wealth, income and other amenities.

(d) Changes in the socio-political structure reflected in changes in the extent to which rural people at the village, area and national level participate in the decision making process.

(e) Changes in the degree and extent of mobility in the class structure of the rural community reflected in allocations of positions of prestige, power and status on the basis of achievement.

(f) Changes in the beliefs, values, attitudes in favour of controlling the *micro* and *macro environment* that mediate change to modern values from traditional ones.

There are no exact criteria to define a village, say as distinct from a small rural town, but there are differences between the two. One such difference is that the village is more closely related to its immediate environment and surroundings than a town. There are also no clear-cut definitions of what constitutes a rural area in both the developed and the developing countries. For simplicity, rural area can be referred to a geographical area away from large urban settlements and towns which is inhabited by rural people. In rural areas, houses and dwelling places are more concentrated around a central 'village', 'square', 'common', 'market place', or 'main street'. Villages or rural areas can also exist on waterways, canals and river tributaries. Thus many fishing villages in tropical countries of Asia and Africa are considered rural. Isolated and scattered herdsmen with sheep, goats and cattle, in many parts of the world live in remote dwelling places. All these serve to illustrate that rural areas and villages can take many forms, shapes and characteristics in different parts of the world.

One may therefore conclude that rural development has varied dimensions and orientations and approaches to rural development also vary from country to country and from time to time.

The original mandate of BARD

Against the backdrop of the preceding definitions of rural people, rural areas and rural development, the approaches and experiences of Comilla Academy (BARD) can be appreciated in the context of the original mandate of BARD and the philosophy of its pioneers, especially that of the first Director, Dr Akhtar Hameed Khan. Originally, BARD (as well as PARD in Peshawar) was to train only the supervisors and development officials of the V-AID Organization. The activities gradually expanded to include training of supervisory and administrative personnel in the civil and other nation-building departments. Later, BARD identified the following functions (BARD, 1993) as part of its mandate:

(a) to train officers in rural development work
(b) to conduct social and economic research and surveys
(c) to undertake model extension activities
(d) to conduct model training classes for villagers
(e) to prepare rural training materials
(f) to discover effective teaching methods
(g) to organize small pilot projects
(h) to evaluate the effectiveness of Academy's operations in small areas.

From the very beginning the role charted by Dr Khan for the Academy was very clear: 'to carry out systematically the experimental planning in our area' and 'to be a living centre of village development, where knowledge is not only collected and disseminated, but some fresh and critical thinking is done, and ideas and schemes are analyzed and tested as in a laboratory' (Khan, 1960, 3-4).

The Comilla model therefore emerged out of a series of experimental projects conducted in Kotwali Thana, the laboratory area of BARD. Dr Khan's view of the scope and methodology of social research was the guiding force behind the Comilla approach as he said,

> I pointed out that academic credibility was not our goal. Our goal was purely utilitarian, viz.; to find a workable model for the departments and then evaluate and refine it further, if it was widely introduced. As the proof of the pudding is in eating, the worth of the pilot project model is in its duplication (Khan, 1991, 24-25).

Thus Dr Khan clearly made a distinction between three kinds of research in the field of rural development: survey, observational and action;

the first was required to be methodologically rigorous, the latter two, not so. The philosophical underpinnings of the Comilla model was to bring about 'security of survival' for all human beings, especially the rural people. Often, other rural development strategies now in vogue erode whatever 'security of survival' the rural people have.

There have been many approaches to rural development such as: bureaucratic approach, technocratic approach, Gandhian-Utopian approach, Missionary approach, Radical approach etc. in the subcontinent. The Comilla approach was not based on the earlier approaches and experiments, rather it was based on 'pragmatism'. Dr Khan's approach was to mesh ideology and humanism to action; and *people* became the most important factor in the Comilla approach.

The concepts of 'people's participation' was in-built to all the activities of BARD; training, research and experimental projects. In fact, the concept went beyond mere participation, and included the internal dynamics of the society. Therefore the issues of access to resources by the rural people, the empowerment and management of the activities by the beneficiaries and evaluation all were present in the Comilla approach. For example, when the two-tier cooperative was introduced, it was criticized from an egalitarian point of view. Dr Khan was quite aware of this fact. He said 'theoretically, the egalitarian argument was irrefutable. Even Mao Tse Tung had accepted agricultural cooperatives as a "mid-way house" or semi-socialism. It is a pity that the purists of Bangladesh did not possess his patience or realism' (Khan, 1984, p. 195, Vol II).

What is the Comilla approach

Approach

The most important element of the Comilla approach to rural development is the creation of an institutional base in rural society to serve as the central focus of basic development programmes. The four major components were:

- A two-tier cooperative system with the primary societies at village level (KSS) and central association at Thana level (TCCA).

- A reorganized rural administration system and local government institutions for coordinating the development activities of the nation building departments operating at the Thana level.

- The Thana Training and Development Centre (TTDC) as an institutional mechanism for coordinating and meeting the training requirements for planning and implementation of development programmes through the officials as well as the institutions and leaders of local governments.

- Infrastructure development programme - the Rural Works Programme (RWP) and the Thana Irrigation Programme (TIP), the two model components of collaborative efforts of the local people, local government and nation building departments.

The essence of these components of the Comilla model was to bring about a change in the rural economy, basically through the principle of people's participation and self reliance. The TTDC was an attempt to provide a decentralized and coordinated institutional base for local level planning and human resource development. All services and supplies and technical expertise were made available at one place for the convenience of the people. The Rural Works Programme (RWP) had, on the other hand, met the requirements of infrastructure development for productive purposes through local level employment generation under the leadership of local organizations. The Thana Irrigation Programme (TIP) was an attempt to develop and manage irrigation resources by the people themselves. The two-tiered cooperatives, on the other hand, were an attempt to organize small farmers through resource mobilization by way of thrift and help them to improve their production potential by promoting managerial and technical skill through training. Thus the ultimate aim was to take the poorer farming population out of the clutches of moneylenders and introduce the spirit of self-financing and self-management among them (Sen, 1992).

All these components were mutually interdependent signifying the multi faceted characteristics of the rural development process. It was made very clear that the programme should be implemented around a common thread the two-tiered cooperative structure. While the cooperative will mobilize resources and provide the technological base for modernizing farming methods through the TTDC; the RWP and TIP would develop the productive capacity of the land and increase income earning opportunities of the poorer villagers in the process. Thus the Comilla model, became a precursor to the integrated rural development movement of the sixties, long before the international agencies became involved in this approach.

Some experiences

The Comilla experiment had established a number of learning experiences, which have been instrumental in shaping the rural development process of Bangladesh. Firstly, it offered an alternative to the bureaucratic model with the introduction of *decentralized administrative structure* for organizing participatory rural development. Secondly, it had shown an effective way of tackling chronic problems of low productivity, food deficit, unemployment and growing poverty in the rural areas. Thirdly, it demonstrated a viable method of *organizing villagers*, self mobilization of resources and ensuring participation in planning and implementation of development programmes. All these learning experiences led the government to adopt the four major programs, viz. the TTDC, RWP, TIP and TCCA, for replication throughout the country.

However, in the course of time, some criticisms were raised against the Comilla approach. The broad thrust of such criticisms was that the model did not address structural change in rural society by altering the land-man relations. While the benefits of development were reaped by the well-to-do farmers due to their better resource endowments, it did not really bring about economic self-reliance, so vital for the sustainability of any rural development strategy. But the fact remains that, no other model of rural development so far had secured the involvement of the farming population themselves like the Comilla approach had done among the villagers across the country including Comilla. This demonstrates the effectiveness of the basic principles behind the model.

Evolution of the Comilla Model

Several elements were combined and steps involved in the evolution of what is now known as the Comilla Approach or the Comilla Models (Sattar, 1993).

The first step taken in setting up the pilot projects was the establishment of a training and research institution - the Academy.

The second step involved was the affiliation of a laboratory area, a whole thana, to this institution. The purpose of the laboratory area was to carry on survey research and organize action-research or pilot projects.

The third step, and a very important one, was thorough study of the laboratory area and *intensive consultation* with the villagers regarding their problems and their views about the solutions to those problems.

The fourth step was close collaboration with the National Planning Commission which formulated and evaluated policies and established priorities in respect of plans and projects.

The fifth was continuous evaluation and documentation of the pilot projects, not only to determine their progress but also to discover their weakness and revise them as and wherever necessary.

The sixth step was providing assistance to government agencies in the replication of the model to other districts.

These are the vital elements, the combination of which led to the development and dissemination of the Comilla Model.

Major hypotheses

There are certain major hypotheses which underpin the development of the Comilla Model. These may be restated as follows:

(a) The villagers have the best understanding of the problems of rural life and the rural environment, so the problems of rural development should be approached from their point of view.

(b) The villagers are capable of bringing about changes in their conditions. Given the means for development (such as creation of capital, provision of training, technical inputs etc.) the villagers themselves would be in a position to initiate the process of change.

(c) Rural development is undoubtedly much wider and broader in scope and dimension than agricultural development. But agricultural development should be made an essential step in initiating a broader rural development process.

(d) The village should be approached as a basic development unit (BDU) and recognized as the starting point for the process of modernization.

(e) Training, research and demonstration are essential in promoting rural development, and these should have symbiotic relations with the life of the rural community.

Empowerment and development

Empowerment is regarded as a process which enables individuals or groups to change balances of power in social, economic and political relations in a society. It refers to many activities, including but not confined to awareness of the societal forces which oppress people and to actions which change power relationships (UNDP, Dhaka 1994).

Empowerment can be viewed at two levels: individual and community level. At the individual level the relevant issues are: patron-client relationship; gender dimension; access to state, market and common property resources. At the community level the principal issues are: the institutional framework, resource mobilization and linkages with other administrative levels of the country (Union, Thana, District etc.).

For empowerment broadly three types of interventions are required which are shown in a systems framework of rural development in Bangladesh below.

Figure 6.1
A systems framework of rural development in Bangladesh

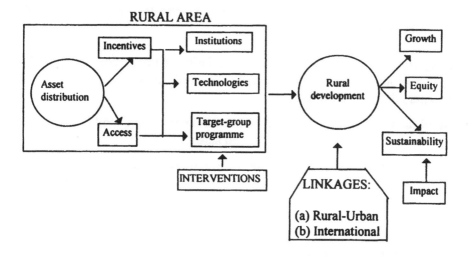

We have outlined above the essence of institutional interventions of the Comilla approach. The technological interventions, in agriculture, livestock, fishery and non-farm activities were also replicated all over Bangladesh. BARD has also been experimenting with target-group programmes such as the Small Farmers Development Programme (SFDP) and Comprehensive Village Development Programme (CVDP), which are described below.

Small Farmers Development Project (SFDP)

Objectives of the project   The small Farmers and the Landless Labourers Development Project (popularly known as SFDP) has been implemented in Bangladesh in 21 thanas (sub-districts) in seven districts since July 1988 with the following objectives:

(a)   To organize the rural poor into small informal groups and to encourage them to undertake income raising activities and thereby to bring the rural poor into a receiving system. The size of each group is between 5 to 7 members.

(b)   To help the target population produce more per unit of their resources.

(c)   To assist the rural poor by inculcating the habit of savings and to build their own capital for investment in income generating activities.

(d)   To link the target population with the delivery system, and to make necessary adjustments in the delivery system to suit the needs of the rural poor.

Beneficiaries of the project   The beneficiaries of the project are identified as two groups of rural poor, namely the small farmers and the landless labourers defined as follows:

Small farmers: Families owning cultivable land between 0.51 and - 1.50 acres.

Landless labourers: Families who do not have any cultivable land, and the families owning a maximum of 0.50 acre of cultivable land (in both cases they may or may not possess homesteads).

Strategy of project implementation   The major strategies followed in the Project, particularly for the achievement of the two main objectives of building capital through savings and earning income through investment of credit, are as follows:

(a)   *Steps towards promotion of savings*
  (i)   Weekly deposits of saving in the group accounts is made mandatory;
  (ii)   The rate of savings per member per week is decided by the group members;

(iii) Savings are usually non-withdrawable except on emergency needs;

(iv) Savings from multiple sources, such as in-kind savings, portion of credit amount, savings from profit money etc. are encouraged;

(v) Savings are put into time series deposits to earn higher profits.

(b) *Steps towards credit operation*

(i) A credit capital fund is developed with resources from UNCDF and Janata Bank at the ratio of 1:2 respectively. The fund is utilized to advance *collateral free loans* to the project beneficiaries against group production plans;

(ii) The credit fund is placed at the Janata Bank (a nationalized commercial bank) Headquarters, and separate allotment is given to each project area. The allotted amount is treated as the revolving fund;

(iii) Only one loan is granted to a group. If an individual member in a group repays the loan early, he/she can receive another loan, provided the group does not default;

(iv) Each successive loan to a group is conditional on a proportionate increase of savings;

(v) Repayment of loans is made by weekly/fortnightly/monthly instalments.

(c) *Organizational arrangement*

In each thana, one Assistant Project Director (APD) with a post-graduate degree is posted. He is supported by a small number of office staff. The APD is empowered to engage rural youths on a temporary basis to work as Group Organizers (GOs) to do the necessary field work. The GOs are paid every month on performance basis. In December 1993, there were 161 GOs and 28 Field Assistants (FAs) for supervising the works of GOs.

(d) *Job responsibilities of the field functionaries*

The APD provides guidance to the FAs and GOs, supervises their activities and maintains liaison with the line agencies particularly with the Bank for overall coordination of the project activities. The GOs conduct the village surveys (to identify the beneficiaries), form informal groups, encourage group members for promotion of savings, channel credit from Banks for various income generating activities, ensure proper utilization and repayment of credit etc.

Each GO looks after an average of 25 groups consisting of 120-150 households.

(e) *Procedure for project implementation*
For successful implementation of the project activities a system has been developed to prepare and update a 'Work manual' that highlights the project implementation procedures. Updating is done on an annual basis through workshops attended by the project personnel, bank officials and project beneficiaries. General contents of the 'Work manual' include the following:

(i) Initial project activities e.g. selection of village, survey and identification of target households;
(ii) Group formation, management and activities;
(iii) Group capital formation;
(iv) Credit programme delineating general principles of credit distribution, assessment of credit worthiness, terms and obligations of credit, mode of credit approval and disbursement, credit supervision and recovery etc.; and
(v) Implementation, monitoring and evaluation modalities of the project.

(f) *Training for field functionaries and beneficiaries*
The project organizes various training activities, orientation courses, workshops, seminars etc., for project personnel, bank officials and beneficiaries mostly related to project implementation. These are held mainly in the field, but in some cases for more interaction with groups of other areas and greater exposure, the orientation courses/workshops are also arranged on the BARD Campus in Comilla.

(g) *Monitoring and evaluation*
An exhaustive proforma has been developed to record the monthly progress of the project activities. These reports are discussed in the coordination meetings held on a rotational basis in each thana with all APDs and representatives of Janata Bank. In addition, the APDs hold monthly meetings in respective thana with project and Bank staff.

(h) *Graduation of groups*
Based on the slogan 'equalize your savings to the amount of credit', an initial ceiling for accumulation of per capita saving has been fixed at Tk. 3,000. Till June 1992, a total of 57 members belonging

to 10 groups in 5 thanas of 3 districts have achieved the target. These group members have been awarded prizes and certificates in a public ceremony. With the achievement of financial viability of the group members, attempts are made to involve them in other aspects of development like education, health etc.

Progress of project activities

The progress of the project activities during July 1988 to July 1993 can be seen in Table 6.1 below.

Table 6.1 Progress of SDP from July 1988 to March 1994

a)	Number of districts	7
b)	Number of Thanas	21
c)	Number of villages	443
d)	Number of groups	4,178
	1) Small Farmers (SF)	1,872
	2) Landless (LL)	2,306
e)	Number of groups by sex	
	1) Male (M)	2,265
	2) Female (F)	1,913
f)	Number of members	24,065
	1) SF	10,789
	2) LL	13,276
g)	Number of members by sex	
	1) M	12,575
	2) F	11,490
h)	Amount of Saving (M.Tk.)	15.03
	1) SF	5.67
	2) LL	9.36
i)	Amount of Saving (M. Tk.) by sex	
	1) M	8.22
	2) F	6.81
j)	Amount of credit by sex	67.29
	1) Disbursed (M. Tk.)	37.39
	M	29.90
	F	43.87
	2) Recovered including interest (M. Tk.)	
	M	24.35
	F	19.52
	3) Overdue (M. Tk.)	0.37
	4) Outstanding (M. Tk.)	25.99
k)	Number of loan recipient	
	1) Groups	3,852
	2) Members	20,541
l)	Percentage of recovery*	
	1) M	98.90
	2) F	99.53

*   Calculated as <u>Recovered amount</u> x 100
                        Recovered amount + Overdue

Jahanara Begum: A Story of Change

Jahanara is a housewife of a poor and landless family in the remote Kalapara thana of Patuakhali district, located in the south of Bangladesh, near the Bay of Bengal. Jahanara had a happy life with her husband, a son and three daughters. Her husband was the only earning member of the family. But misery befell on her when her husband threw her and four children out of the house on a false accusation that she had an illicit relationship with another man. Jahanara first went to her widow mother who was merely a maid-servant. So, Jahanara with her family and her mother were left to fend for themselves. Jahanara started supplying 50 pitchers of water to a shop and earned only Taka 150 (roughly US$ 4) per month. Then she took up another additional job of cleaner and earned a total of Tk. 400 per month. She could barely survive with her family and sometimes was compelled to beg from others. Then she came across the project person of SFDP and became interested in joining the project. She started coming to SFDP office and also attended group meetings as an observer. After completing some official formalities, she joined a group in June 1990 named "Natun Bazar Bhumiheen Mahila Group No. 1", with seven female members from landless families.

The group opened a bank account with the Janata Bank and began to deposit their savings regularly. After seven months the group saved a total of Tk. 2,000. During that time the observation period of 6 months was over and the group applied for its first loan. Janata Bank sanctioned a loan of Tk. 18,000 out of which Jahanara received Tk. 3,000. With that amount she bought a second-hand rickshaw (three-wheeler) and rented it out to her brother at a rate of Tk. 50 per day. Thus she started earning Tk. 1,500 per month, out of which she used to deposit Tk. 200 as monthly instalment for loan repayment. Within four months the living condition of her family members improved dramatically. She got her daughters admitted into a school. Not only that, she bought a pair of golden earrings for herself which gave her immense pride of possession. She has never defaulted to repay her loan and she has a plan to buy another rickshaw after full repayment of her first loan.

Jahanara has attained the knack of entrepreneurship and has become confident and optimistic about her life. She is no longer a burden on her mother, rather she extends financial help to her old mother. Her own saving with the Janata Bank has reached Tk. 1,000. With beaming smile she once said to a SFDP project person, "Sir, SFDP has really given me a new life". Jahanara is a living case of success of *women's empowerment* under the aegis of the Comilla approach in the present context of Bangladesh.

Source: Case Study by Abul Kashem, SFDP
            Newsletter (BARD), October, 1992, Vol. 2.

Comprehensive Village Development Programme (CVDP)

Objectives of CVDP: During the late 1970s BARD started an experimental project entitled 'Total Village Development Project (TVDP)' in its laboratory area of Comilla Kotwali thana. Based on the experiences of this project BARD started CVDP in 1983 in other areas of Comilla. In 1991 CVDP was started within the framework of the Fourth Five Year Plan of Bangladesh. BARD is now implementing this experimental project in forty villages of Comilla Sadar (Kotwali), Burichang, Sylhet Sadar and Sonargaon thanas which are situated in three districts. The Rural Development Academy (RDA) located in Bogra district, another institution like BARD, has been given the responsibility of implementing CVDP in forty villages of four thanas in four districts located in northern part of Bangladesh. The general objective of the programme is to improve the socio-economic condition and quality of life of all groups of people in the village through a common institutional framework. The specific objectives of CVDP as embodied in the Fourth Five Year Plan are to:

(a) develop common village facilities and make available at the village level various social and economic services relating to literacy and education, population control and family planning, minimum health care and nutrition, income generating activities and others;

(b) increase production in both farm and non-farm sectors, expand productive employment and household income utilizing all available resources;

(c) encourage capital formation in the cooperative society;

(d) develop human resources;

(e) ensure the equitable distribution of benefits of development to all.

Institutional arrangements   In each village, there is a village-based Cooperative called the Comprehensive Village Development Cooperative Society (CVDCs). It envisages to cover all the villagers under the broad categorization of adult males, adult females and children. The members if the first two groups are again divided into a number of small functional groups. The CVDCSs are managed by a Managing Committee (MC) having a proportionate representation from each functional group except that of the children.

The representatives for the MC are directly elected by the adult members of the CVDCSs. The CVDCSs devote all their activities to become an economically viable and self-reliant institution by means of resource mobilization through small savings and by undertaking various productive and commercial business activities within the disciplines of cooperatives. The existing cooperative societies and informal groups in the project villages will be gradually amalgamated with the CVDCSs depending on their financial status. No new cooperative society and group other than CVDCSs will be promoted in those villages.

In parallel, the CVDCSs will have links to their thana level cooperative associations. The other linkage of CVDCSs will be with local government bodies at different tiers and thana level nation building departments, the purpose of which will be to develop common village facilities and services (physical, social and economic), and obtaining support services available at the union, thana and districts.

BARD has so far organized 23 CVDCSs in Comilla (Sadar and Burichang thanas), 10 in Sylhet Sadar and another 7 in Sonargaon thana of Narayanganj.

As far as the membership coverage and capital formation is concerned (up to June 1993), 40 CVDCSs enlisted 10,061 members representing 4,163 male, 2,371 female and 3,527 children. Total accumulated capital stands at Tk.1,03,39,538 as share and savings. Eight out of 40 societies had so far enlisted 100 per cent of the village families and rest of the societies are progressing towards that end. The average family coverage in each of the 40 CVDCSs now stands at around 54 per cent; out of a total 8,104 families, 4,400 accepted membership of the societies.

All the Comilla societies finance 60 per cent of credit operation from their own resources. By August 1993 all the 40 societies of Comilla, Sonargaon and Sylhet districts have prepared their Village Resources Books on the basis of which they started formulating their Comprehensive Village Development Plans.

So far, on the basis of the Resource Books, Comilla societies had implemented 11 and Sylhet societies 3 such Annual Development Plans (ADP) up to July 1993. The project activities in Sonargaon has started only in September 1992. They formulated their first Annual Village Development Plans for the year 1993-94.

As poverty is not a uni-dimensional problem, there is no short-cut method to resolve it. The CVDP is an experiment in creating institutional infrastructure to address rural problems of socio-economic development. Unlike may target-group oriented programme, the CVDP emphasizes more on productive options to resolve poverty issues. It discourages soft options/relief orientations in addressing poverty or any other specific problem associated with rural development.

It encourages *self-management* by promoting local leadership and community spirit on the one hand, and helps to form collective capital through regular small savings. It does not isolate the rich and the poor and divide men and women but the poor and the women get special attention in the process of implementation of the programme.

A notable feature of the CVDP project is to utilize the services of a nationalized commercial bank, the *Sonali Bank*, in the credit operation of the project. An amount of Tk. 1 million has been kept in the project as the 'seed money' to be used as a revolving fund to provide credit to the needy people from the project itself. According to a Memorandum of Understanding (MOU) between *BARD* and the *Sonali Bank*, the said amount has been kept in one year fixed deposit with the Bank. The bank will provide a loan up to 80 percent of the said amount to the target groups at the rate fixed by the Bangladesh Central Bank. In the credit operation, however, the bulk of the fund comes from the savings and share capital of the members of the cooperative societies themselves.

The progress in terms of some indicators can be seen in Table 6.2. It should be remembered that unlike SFDP, this project (CVDP) does not have the major focus on credit operation. Therefore, Table 6.2 does not give the overall achievement of the project, it just gives information on selected indicators.

Table 6.2 Progress of CVDP up to July 1994

a)	Number of districts	3
b)	Number of Thanas	4
c)	Number of cooperative societies	40
d)	Number of families covered	5,275
e)	Number of members	11,302
	1) Male	4,615
	2) Female	2,820
	3) Young (age 5-17)	3,867
f)	Capital formation (M.Tk.)	17.28
	1) Savings deposits	3.83
	Male	1.69
	Female	.85
	Young	1.29
	2) Share capital (M.Tk.)	7.54
	Male	5.78
	Female	1.76
	3) Other deposits (M.Tk.)	5.91
g)	Credit operation	
	1) *From societies' own fund*	
	- Loan given (M.Tk.)	3.80
	- Loan recovered (M.Tk.)	1.88
	-Percentage of Loan recovery	49.5
	2) *From external sources*	
	- Loan given (M.Tk.)	3.65
	- Loan recovered (M.Tk.)	2.04
	- Percentage of Loan recovery	55.90
	3) Seed capital of CVDP (M.Tk.)	1.00
	Loan given out of seed capital (M.Tk.)	0.79

*   Calculated as $\dfrac{\text{Recovered amount}}{\text{Recovered amount} + \text{Overdue}} \times 10$

Empowerment through Skill Development:
A Tale of Seven Women

Seven women from landless families from seven villages in Sonargaon thana of Narayanganj district were classic examples of deprivation and poverty of the womenfolk in Bangladesh.

Setara is a widow with two children. She was thrown out from her husband's house after her husband's death. She went to her poor parents. Hasna, Hosne Ara, Shamsun (1) and Shamsun (2) are all married but their living conditions were deplorable. Nazneen and Kohinoor are unmarried and they were burdens on their families. CVDP with its diverse clientele profile brought these seven women into the mainstream of development. All these seven women are now members of seven Comprehensive Village Cooperative Societies since their formation in September 1992.

These women received training in a two-month cutting-sewing course arranged by BARD in Comilla city. Along with cutting and sewing of clothes, these women, among others, were also trained in management and accounting aspects of cooperative societies and informal groups. They were also exposed to other women cooperative members of Comilla and elsewhere. They received training on their positions in the society, their own problems and their hidden potentials to change for a better life. Hasna, Hosne Ara, Shamsun (1) and Shamsun (2) each of them now earns Tk.500-700 per month from sewing and each of them own one sewing machine costing Tk.1,200-2,000. These women are also training other women in their respective villages.

Setara is now earning a good amount of money from her sewing works. She has vindicated her honour which is reflected in the fact that the family of her dead husband now respects her and Setara has been gladly accepted by her husband's family where she is living now. Nazneen, even though she is unmarried, now contributes Tk.500-700 per month to incur the expenses of her joint-family with 16 members. Nazneen is regarded now as some sort of a saviour of her family. Kohinoor is now a respected young lady who has become a highly sought after bride by many families. Now there is no demand for a dowry from the prospective bridegrooms' families.

> These seven women, through CVDP of BARD have become good examples of women's empowerment through skill development and income generating activities. Their achievements in terms of quantitative indicators like income and employment may be modest, but the qualitative changes which have come to their lives are quite significant. The diverse situations and achievements of the seven women have one common theme: empowerment of the poor can be achieved through motivation, hard work, support services, and skill development resulting in the ultimate goal of higher productivity and income. Above all, what is required is an institutional approach instead of an ad hoc piece-meal approach, and that is what CVDP is all about.

Source: Case Study by Tofail Ahmed and A.B.M. Shahidullah, BARD, January 1994.

Based on the previous experience, a special project 'Local Level Planning and Management Project' was initiated by BARD in 1989 with funds from the Asia Foundation, under which a series of vertically integrated training programmes for village cooperative leaders, Union Parishad Chairmen, officials and public representatives were conducted. The training programmes were evaluated by a Committee of experts which suggested that a manual should be prepared to facilitate implementation of such training programmes in other areas of Bangladesh. In this context another project entitled 'Local Level Planning and Management: Preparation of Manual and Training of Functionaries' was taken up by BARD in 1993 with funds from the Asia Foundation. The major purpose of the project was to prepare a comprehensive manual on local level planning and management and organize five training courses for village leaders, Union Parishad members and field level development workers in four thanas of three districts namely: Narayanganj, Sylhet and Comilla. The training courses, each of one week duration, were held at the local level where experts were taken, and a total of 143 people attended in five courses. On the basis of these courses a draft manual entitled '*Local Level Planning and Management*' has been prepared. To give the manual a final shape, a two-day workshop and a two-day seminar were organized by BARD on two different occasions. The draft manual is now being finalized on the basis of the recommendations of the workshop and the seminar. The manual will be mainly in Bengali language and an English version will also be prepared. This particular exercise of BARD will help the local communities and the government, which has recently embarked upon a process of participatory bottom-up planning to prepare a pragmatic five year micro development plan for Bangladesh.

Conclusion

The global and the national contexts have changed. One might ask whether in that context the Comilla approach is still viable. In the wake of NGO activities and demand for a Pro-poor Plan in Bangladesh, the relevance of the Comilla approach and experiences should not be overlooked.

To be effective, a rural development strategy should comprise certain essential elements. These elements are people's participation in the development process, decentralized decision-making, institution building and development of people's organization, development of human resources and skills, internalization of innovations, mobilization and use of local resources, linkages of people's organizations with public sector and other institutions, production and employment generation, and sustainability of development. The Comilla approach contains all these elements.

People often criticize the Comilla approach on the basis of the problems associated with its implementation all over the country. Different organizations like the Bangladesh Rural Development Board (BRDB), the Bangladesh Agricultural Development Corporation (BADC), the Local Government Engineering Department (LGED) were all responsible for implementing various components of the Comilla model. Often there was a lack of coordination among all these organizations which made a comprehensive package like the Comilla model, a mix of several disjointed efforts. Sometimes, people associate the Comilla model with BRDB and attribute BRDB's problems to the Comilla model, which is not justifiable. Moreover, BRDB implements only one component, that is, the two-tier cooperative system (TCCA) of the Comilla model. That too has enjoyed some success despite what many sceptics may think. The minor irrigation scheme, rural infrastructure development and conscious raising of development institutions are all examples of successes of the Comilla approach. In a recent SAARC/World Bank meeting (October, 1993), it was observed that 'South Asia can boast of having led the world in the development of community-based organizations; it has a rich tradition of grassroots participation dating back at least to the Independence movement... Bangladesh has been the home of three of the best-known programmes of this type: the Comilla model of linked farmer's cooperatives, the Grameen Bank's targeted credit programme, and the integrated development approach of the Bangladesh Rural Advancement Committee (BRAC)'. In fact, the Comilla model was the pioneer of all the rural development efforts in Bangladesh including those of the Grameen Bank and BRAC mentioned in the above quotation. It was the Comilla approach which provided the intellectual impetus and operational dimensions to the concepts like 'conscientization', 'participation', and 'empowerment' of the rural poor. The current vitality of poverty reducing programmes in Bangladesh owe much to the research and innovations developed painstakingly at Comilla.

Note

1.   The views expressed here are the author's own.

References

Ahmed, Salehuddin (1991), 'Concept Paper on Orientation and Approaches to Rural Development Enterprise', Paper for the Faculty Development Programme of the Project Development Institute, Development Academy of the Philippines (DAP), Quezon City.

Ahmed, Tofail (1993), 'Comprehensive Village Development Programme', *The Bangladesh Observer*, Dhaka, 13 November.

BARD, (1993), 'A Master Plan of Socio-Economic Research at Bangladesh Academy for Rural Development', prepared under the Assistance to the Development of BARD Project.

Bari, Fazlul (1993), 'Small Farmer Development Project (SFDP) in Bangladesh', in *Poverty Focused Rural Development*, Ed. M.A. Quddus, BARD, Comilla.

Khan Akhter Hameed (1960), Director's Speech, *First Annual Report*, Comilla, Pakistan Academy for Village Development.

Khan Akhter Hameed (1984), *Works of Akhter Hameed Khan*, Vol. III, BARD, Kotbari, Comilla.

Khan Akhter Hameed (1991), 'My Development Education', *Asia-Pacific Journal of Rural Development*, Vol. 1, No. 2.

Poostchi, Iraj (1986), *Rural Development and the Developing Countries: an Interdisciplinary Introductory Approach*, Alger Press, Oshawa, Canada.

Sattar, M.G. (1993), 'Comilla Models of Rural Development: Significance and Relevance' in *Rural Development in Bangladesh*, Ed. M.A. Quddus, BARD, Comilla.

Sen, Dibyendu (1992), 'Rural Development Strategies and Experiences in Bangladesh: Some Issues', Paper at the International Seminar on Rural Development in Bangladesh, BARD, Comilla, 15-17 January, 1992.

SAARC/World Bank Informal Workshop (1993), 'Poverty Reduction in South Asia: Promoting Participation by the Poor', Summary Report; October 12-16, Annapolis, Maryland, USA.

UNDP, Dhaka (1994), 'Empowerment of Women', UNDP's 1994 Report on Human Development in Bangladesh, Dhaka.

Webster, R.L. (1975), *Integrated Communication*, East-West Communication Institute, East-West Center, University of Hawaii.

7 Poverty Reduction Strategies in Malaysia, 1971-1995: Major Features

FADIL AZIM ABBAS

Introduction

This paper highlights the major features of the progress made by Malaysia in poverty reduction since 1971. It also includes an analysis of the possible reasons for the achievements.

The chapter is divided into three main sections, namely:-

- The enabling environment for poverty reduction.
- Poverty reduction: Policy, Achievements and Future Challenges.
- Some possible lessons from the Malaysian experience.

The enabling environment for poverty reduction

The efforts of Malaysia in reducing poverty has been conducted against the backdrop of a plural society that has as its ultimate goal the establishment of a united Malaysian nation from amongst its many ethnic groups. This goal, which has enjoyed the acceptance of all ethnic groups, has circumscribed and influenced the thinking and action on all important social problems in Malaysia, including those pertaining to poverty. As such, efforts at dealing with them have acquired an added urgency. In this regard, Malaysia has been fortunate to have acquired the necessary and sufficient range of factors to enable policies that deal with poverty, to achieve notable levels of success and thereby contributed towards building the foundation of national unity. The factors are interrelated in a complex network of causes and effects but, for purpose of analysis, can be categorized into the following major ones, namely:-

- A plural society living in peaceful co-existence and harmony.
- Government fully committed to socio-economic development.
- Rapid and continuous economic growth.

A Plural Society Living in Peaceful Co-existence and Harmony

Malaysia's plural society has found a formula for peaceful co-existence and harmonious multi-ethnic and multi-faith living. Its main ingredients are as follows:-

(a) Those involved in the drafting of the Federal Constitution were mindful of the potentially explosive nature of ethnic relations, have wisely entrenched in it provisions which authorise Parliament to legislate against, *inter alia*, people who promote feelings of ill-will and hostility between different races or other classes of the population that are likely to cause violence;

(b) The relevant government agencies have managed to avert ethnic tension from transforming itself into ethnic violence, almost without fail;

(c) The curriculum of the public education system has been developed not only to prepare the young for the demands of the job market but also to instil in them a set of common values and a sense of being Malaysian; and

(d) Most importantly, ethnic groups in Malaysia have demonstrated a strong preference for negotiation and accommodation rather than open confrontation to resolve ethnic differences. A clear indication of this is the repeated victory, in every general election since 1955, of the Alliance Party and then its successor the National Front, both coalitions of ethnic parties that have consistently emphasized consultation and compromise on ethnic issues. The continuing support for them has not only reduced publicised and politicised debates on ethnic issues thus avoiding potential conflict but has also produced political stability and allowed ethnic leaders who believe in consultation and compromise to work together as national leaders and Cabinet colleagues in the overall development of Malaysia.

The net result of these efforts have been to reduce ethnic tensions and violence. In its place, peaceful co-existence among the ethnic groups has enabled Malaysians to direct and concentrate their resources on economic and social development.

A government fully committed to socio-economic development

Reflecting the preference of Malaysians in general, the government has subscribed strongly to the belief that economic development if it is to be really meaningful and sustained, must involve and accrue to all citizens, including the poor, unemployed, marginalized communities and generally, the disadvantaged groups. This philosophy of development, i.e. growth with equity, is embodied in all major public policies of Malaysia. Among them, three can be regarded as being the most important, viz. the New Economic Policy (NE), the National Development Policy (NDP) and Vision 2020.

The NEP (1971-1990) The NEP, which was in force between 1971 and 1990, was the product of pragmatic thinking on the desirable direction of national development, i.e. *growth with equity* and active government participation in the economy and not maximum growth through a *laissez faire* or free market economic system. It was born out of a realization that the *laissez faire* system which was in place since Independence in 1957 and whose shortcomings were a major contributing factor to the tragic but fortunately short-lived ethnic riots in 1969, was inadequate and incongruous for a plural society in which different ethnic groups were at different levels of economic development. A policy of total *laissez faire* would only exacerbate entrenched group differences, create resentment among those left behind by the forces of growth and eventually lead to a breakdown in social cohesion. This could only be counterbalanced by a certain degree of government intervention to ensure equitable growth. Thus, the Malaysian government introduced the NEP, which was, at the time, viewed by some pro-market economists with apprehension.

The NEP had as its goal *national unity*, i.e. a condition in which all Malaysians have willingly accepted that loyalty and dedication to the nation override all other loyalties. To achieve this goal, two major strategies were utilised, predicated upon the premise that national unity is unattainable without greater equity and balance among Malaysia's ethnic and other social groups in their participation in the development of the country. It was understood that national unity could not be fostered if vast sections of the population remain poor and if sufficient productive employment opportunities are not created for the expanding labour force.

105

The two strategies were:-

(a) reducing absolute poverty with the intention of eventually eradicating it, by raising income levels and increasing employment opportunities for all Malaysians, irrespective of race; and

(b) restructuring society to correct economic imbalances so as to reduce and eventually eliminate the identification of race with economic function.

Another feature of the NEP was that it was predicated upon the assumption of a rapidly growing economy. This was deemed necessary so as to, *inter alia*,

(a) provide the increased employment or economic opportunities for the poor and other disadvantaged groups to enable them to get out of poverty and to participate in the mainstream of economic activities; and

(b) ensure that distribution did not take place from the reallocation of existing wealth but from expanding and new sources of wealth.

The NDP (1991-2000) The NDP, introduced in 1991 as the successor to the NEP as Malaysia's all-encompassing development policy, reaffirmed the relevance of the latter by retaining its main elements. But at the same time, in view of the emergence of fresh challenges, the NDP introduced several new thrusts for *balanced development*. These new thrusts together with the old served to emphasize the growing concern of Malaysians that increasing consideration be given to non-materialistic matters in national development which encompass, among others, the strengthening of social and spiritual values and protection of the environment and ecology. More specifically, they covered the following:-

- striking an optimum balance between the goals of *economic growth* and *equity*;
- ensuring a balanced development of the *major sectors* of the economy so as to increase their mutual complementarities to optimize growth;
- reducing and ultimately eliminating the *social and economic inequalities and imbalances* in the country to promote a fair and more equitable sharing of the benefits of economic growth by all Malaysians;
- promoting and strengthening national integration by reducing the

wide disparities in economic development *between states* and *between the urban and rural areas* in the country;

- developing a progressive society in which all citizens enjoy greater *material welfare*, while simultaneously imbued with positive *social and spiritual values*, and an increased sense of *national pride and consciousness*;
- promoting human resource development including creating a productive and disciplined labour force and developing the necessary skills to meet the challenges in industrial development through a *culture of merit and excellence* without jeopardising the *restructuring objectives*;
- making *science and technology an integral component of socio-economic planning and development*, which entails building competence in strategic and knowledge-based technologies, and promoting a science and technology culture in the process of building a modern industrial economy; and
- ensuring that in the pursuit of *economic development*, adequate attention will be given to the *protection of the environment and ecology* so as to maintain the long-term sustainability of the country's development.

With regard to balancing growth with equity, which was the primary focus of the NEP, the NDP introduced the following shifts in strategies to eradicate poverty and restructure society:-

- shift the focus of the anti-poverty strategy towards eradication of *hardcore* poverty while at the same time reducing relative poverty;
- focus on employment and the rapid development of an active *Bumiputera* Commercial and Industrial Community (BCIC) as a more effective strategy to increase the meaningful participation of the *Bumiputera* in the modern sectors of the economy;
- rely more on the private sector to be involved in the restructuring objective by creating greater opportunities for its growth; and
- focus on human resource development as a fundamental requirement for achieving the objectives of growth and distribution.

Vision 2020

Vision 2020, which is a vision of what Malaysia should be like in the year 2020, has become the basis for planning Malaysia's future. In essence, it calls for *total development* and envisages that, 'By the year 2020, Malaysia can be a united nation, with a confident Malaysian society, infused by strong moral and ethical values, living in a society that is democratic, liberal and tolerant, caring, economically just and equitable, progressive and prosperous and in full possession of an economy that is competitive, dynamic, robust and resilient'.

To realise the Vision, nine strategic challenges will have to be met, namely,

(a) Establishing a united Malaysian nation with a sense of common and shared destiny. This must be a nation at peace with itself, territorially and ethnically integrated, living in harmony and full and fair partnership, made up of one 'Bangsa Malaysia' (Malaysian Society) with political loyalty and dedication to the nation.

(b) Creating a psychologically liberated, secure, and developed Malaysian Society with faith and confidence in itself, justifiably proud of what it is, of what it has accomplished, robust enough to face all manner of adversity. This Malaysian Society must be distinguished by the pursuit of excellence, fully aware of all its potentials, psychologically subservient to none, and respected by the peoples of other nations.

(c) Fostering and developing a mature democratic society, practising a form of mature consensual, community-oriented Malaysian democracy that can be a model for many developing countries.

(d) Establishing a fully moral and ethical society, whose citizens are strong in religious and spiritual values and imbued with the highest of ethical standards.

(e) Establishing a mature, liberal and tolerant society in which Malaysians of all colours and creeds are free to practise and profess their customs, cultures and religious beliefs and yet feeling that they belong to one nation.

(f) Establishing a scientific and progressive society, a society that is innovative and forward-looking, one that is not only a consumer of technology but also a contributor to the scientific and technological civilization of the future.

(g) Establishing a fully caring society and a caring culture, a social system in which society will come before self, in which the welfare of the people will revolve not around the state or the individual but around a strong and resilient family system.

(h) Ensuring an economically-just society. This is a society in which there is a fair and equitable distribution of the wealth of the nation, in which there is full partnership in economic progress. Such a society cannot be in place so long as there is the identification of race with economic function, and the identification of economic backwardness with race.

(i) Establishing a prosperous society, with an economy that is fully competitive, dynamic, robust and resilient.

In effect, Vision 2020 is very much like the NDP and NEP in giving an emphatic focus to the achievement of a suitable balance among competing concerns in development. It manages, however, to add a further humanistic element to the Malaysian concept of development. This element, highlighted in the seventh challenge, stresses the importance of creating a fully caring society and a caring culture based upon a strong and resilient family system which is expected to harbour individuals from the negative effects of development in a more effective way than the government-based social security systems currently employed by many countries.

The idea that development should not be directed solely at maximising economic growth has been an important feature in major Malaysian national development policies. In addition, since its introduction in the NEP, it has been broadened to include not only the need to balance growth with equitable distribution but also a host of other factors. The continuous emphasis given to the above ideal reflects the government's awareness it is something which most Malaysians subscribe to and underlines the government's own commitment to it.

Development expenditure, 1971-1995

To complement the stated policy on distribution and balanced development, the federal government has spent RM37.2 billion on social services between 1971 and 1995, including RM19.9 billion for education and training, RM4.5 billion for health and population (family planning and associated services), RM8.7 billion for public housing (including subsidised housing loans for public service personnel) and almost RM4.0 billion for other services, such as welfare and village and community development (Table 7.1).

The RM37.2 billion represents about 22.6 per cent of the total public development expenditure (RM164.9 billion) of the federal government for the period 1971-95 compared to almost 59 per cent (RM97.2 billion) for the economic sector, 15.5 per cent (RM25.6 billion) for national defence and security and 3.0 per cent (RM5.0 billion) for administration. In this regard, it is worth noting that the 22.6 per cent spent on education, health, public housing and related services is consistent with the 20 per cent currently being recommended by the 20:20 Compact. Further, it should be pointed out too, that a major portion of the expenditure for the economic sector was actually directed at improving transportation (e.g. road and bridge construction, including rural ones), communication (e.g. telecommunications and postal supplies). If they are taken into consideration too, then the total size of public development expenditure spent between 1971 and 1995 to improve the quality of life in Malaysia would be 52.3 per cent or RM86.3 billion.

Rapid and continuous economic growth

A striking feature of Malaysia's development has been the rapid and continuous growth of its economy for almost four decades. Perhaps, even more striking, is the fact that it has been achieved within an environment of price and exchange rate stability.

Malaysia's real Gross Domestic Product (GDP) growth for the NEP period (1971-1990) averaged 6.7 per cent annually, topping the average of 6.0 per cent for the 1960s. The rate picked up further between 1991 and 1995 to reach an annual average of 8.7 per cent.

Table 7.1 Malaysia: Federal Government Development Expenditure, 1971-1995 RM (million)

	1971-75	(%)	1976-80	(%)	1981-85	(%)	1986-90	(%)	1991-95	(%)	1971-95	(%)
Economic	**4,956.42**	**66.8**	**13,570.79**	**64.0**	**28,042.13**	**64.0**	**22,886.90**	**64.8**	**27,712.00**	**50.6**	**97,167.34**	**58.9**
Agriculture and Rural Development	1,793.53	24.2	4,672.41	22.0	7,540.90	16.3	7,325.00	20.8	6,344.00	11.6	27,675.84	16.8
Mineral Resources Development	0.56	0.0	15.70	0.1	27.79	0.1	43.00	0.1	50.00	0.1	137.05	0.1
Commerce & Industry	1,433.20	19.3	3,246.21	15.3	6,308.78	13.6	3,981.00	11.3	4,047.00	7.4	19,016.19	11.5
Transport	1,233.92	16.6	2,842.75	13.4	6,989.69	15.1	6,823.00	19.3	12,270.00	22.4	30,159.36	18.3
Communications	174.93	2.4	1,152.08	5.4	2,422.54	5.2	792.00	2.2	70.00	0.1	4,611.55	2.8
Energy	122.74	1.7	1,205.30	5.7	2,624.13	5.7	918.00	2.6	829.00	1.5	5,699.17	3.4
Water Resources	163.12	2.2	377.22	1.8	1,947.65	4.2	2,667.00	7.6	3,433.00	6.3	8,587.99	5.2
Feasibility Studies	34.42	0.5	59.12	0.3	64.85	0.1	52.00	0.1	99.00	0.2	309.39	0.2
Research/Development	0.00	0.0	0.00	0.0	115.80	0.3	285.00	0.8	570.00	1.0	970.80	0.6
Social	**1,286.74**	**17.4**	**3,635.99**	**17.1**	**9,972.69**	**21.5**	**8,764.00**	**24.8**	**13,555.00**	**24.8**	**37,214.42**	**22.6**
Education & Training	695.92	9.4	1,548.18	7.3	4,687.59	10.1	5,700.00	16.1	7,315.00	13.4	19,946.69	12.1
Health & Population	183.25	2.5	307.40	1.4	736.51	1.6	931.00	2.6	2,387.00	4.4	4,545.16	2.8
Housing & Sewerage	174.61	2.4	1,360.14	6.4	3,934.89	8.5	1,452.00	4.1	1,825.00	3.3	8,746.64	5.3
Related Services	232.96	3.1	420.27	2.0	613.70	1.3	681.00	1.9	2,028.00	3.7	3,975.93	2.4
Security	**1,021.98**	**13.8**	**3,529.80**	**16.7**	**7,494.58**	**16.2**	**2,527.00**	**7.2**	**10,987.00**	**20.1**	**25,560.36**	**15.5**
Administration	**149.95**	**2.0**	**465.32**	**2.2**	**810.60**	**1.8**	**1,123.00**	**3.2**	**2,451.00**	**4.5**	**4,999.87**	**3.0**
Total Expenditure	**7,415.09**	**100.0**	**21,201.90**	**100.0**	**46,320.00**	**100.0**	**35,300.00**	**100.0**	**54,705.00**	**100.0**	**164,941.99**	**100.0**

Source: Economic Planning Unit, Malaysia

111

In absolute terms, the GDP, in constant 1978 prices, grew from RM24.9 billion to RM120.3 billion between 1971 and 1995. In the process, the structure of the economy changed from one dominated by the services and agriculture sectors (36.2 and 29 per cent share of GDP, respectively) in 1970 to one in which manufacturing assumed the second position (33.1 per cent) after services (44.1 per cent) in 1995. In line with the larger contribution of manufacturing to the GDP, its contribution to exports also increased from a mere 11.9 per cent of total export in 1970 to 79.6 per cent in 1995.

Similarly, the Gross National Product (GNP), in constant 1978 prices, grew from RM22.2 billion in 1971 to RM113.5 billion in 1995. Consistent with this growth, per capita GNP, in constant terms, grew by more than nine times, from RM1,109 to RM10,058 over that period. In spite of increased incomes, however, the annual inflation rate has remained low as indicated by the 3.4 per cent growth in 1995 compared to an annual average of 1.6 per cent for the 1970s. Similarly, the Malaysian Ringgit has also remained fairly stable vis-a-vis the US Dollar over the period, having been traded at around RM2.50 to US$1 in 1995 compared to RM3.08 in the 1970s and RM2.22 in the 1980s.

Among the many factors that have contributed toward the achievements of the Malaysian economy, the most significant has been the consistent pragmatism of Malaysia's macro-economic policies. At the broadest level, this has been manifested by the changes introduced to the role of the government in economic development over the years in line with the emergence of new challenges and public demands as well as the acquisition of new ideas on the management of the economy.

In the immediate post-Independence period, the *laissez faire* policy of the British colonial government continued to be followed, although, even then, the national government had begun to play a bigger role in bringing about development, particularly to the rural areas. At the same time, it also promoted the further growth of the tin-mining and rubber-growing industries - the mainstay of the national economy then - as well as stimulated the growth of the nascent manufacturing sector. When this free market approach failed to produce the desired level of participation of the major ethnic group, the Malays or *Bumiputera*, into the mainstream of economic activities, the government gave itself a more direct participatory role in economic and business activities so as to ensure that distributive targets were given due attention. However, by the beginning of 1983, the government had begun to take the first tentative steps to reverse this policy i.e. to reduce its role in the economy and instead assign to the private sector the role of the engine of growth. Thus, a more positive government stance towards business was developed, manifested in the forms of more favourable fiscal policies and other non-fiscal incentives and the stream-lining of rules and regulations.

These efforts were followed by the introduction of the privatization and Malaysia Incorporated policies. The former involved, *inter alia*, the sale of government equity in its companies or the corporization of public agencies prior to its public sale or contracting out work or functions by public agencies and was generally aimed at reducing the government's presence in the economy. The latter policy, Malaysia Inc., patterned along the lines of Japan Inc., was aimed at building and sustaining a close working relationship between the public and private sectors so as to facilitate and stimulate the growth of the latter. Given the more rapid growth that has accompanied the liberalization of the economy, there is a likelihood of further liberalization, particularly if distributional aspects of development are not negatively affected by it.

In terms of effects, the sustained economic growth has led to increasing job and economic opportunities, thereby resulting in increasing incomes. More importantly, because of the stress on growth with distribution in Malaysia, the opportunities have also benefited the *Bumiputera*, the poor and other vulnerable groups. Further, because the stress was also on distribution of new wealth, no group was forcibly deprived of its existing wealth. Thus, the net effect of growth in Malaysia has been increased real incomes for all without creating inter-ethnic conflict or violence.

Poverty eradication: policy, achievements and future challenges

Policy

Malaysia's policy against poverty first took a clear and coordinated shape in 1971 with the introduction of the New Economic Policy (NEP). Since then, its basic features have been retained even though there have been modifications made to it. In other words, poverty eradication has remained as an integral component of major policies such as the NEP, NDP and Vision 2020, signifying the continuing importance attached to it.

113

Concepts and measurements

An important component or prerequisite of the fight against poverty is agreement on the definition and measurement of poverty. In Malaysia, the government has taken the lead in this task, after consultation with various experts and groups. In this regard, three concepts pertaining to poverty have been adopted by Malaysia to circumscribe and underpin its poverty eradication programmes, viz., absolute poverty, absolute hardcore poverty and relative poverty.

Absolute poverty has been defined as a condition in which the gross monthly income of a household is insufficient to purchase certain minimum necessities of life. These necessities include a minimum food basket to maintain household members in good nutritional health and other basic needs, viz., clothing and footwear, rent, fuel and power, transportation and communication, health-care, education and recreation.

To facilitate the measurement of this condition, a poverty line income (PLI) gas been constructed and used based on the basic costs of the items mentioned above. Further, since the PLI is linked to the consumer price index (CPI), the PLI has been periodically revised in line with movements in the CPI. Furthermore, since the cost of living and household size over different parts of Malaysia are not the same, different PLIs and household sizes have been utilized for them (Table 7.2). However, no differentiation has been made with regard to urban and rural PLIs and household size.

Absolute hardcore poverty has been defined as a condition in which the gross monthly income of a household is less than half of the PLI. This definition was introduced in 1988 to enable more accurate targeting of poverty redressal projects to the hardcore poor.

Relative poverty The conceptualization that has been used in Malaysia is linked to the notion of income disparity between groups. Thus, a group whose mean income is less than another has been defined as being in relative poverty. Under this definition, it is possible to define a group, for example rural dwellers, as being in relative poverty to another, urban dwellers, even though their mean income exceeds the PLI.

Table 7.2 Malaysia: Poverty line incomes and household sizes for peninsular Malaysia, Sabah and Sarawak 1990, 1995

	1990		1995	
	RM	HS	RM	HS
Peninsular Malaysia	370	5.14	425	4.6
Sabah	544	5.36	601	4.9
Sarawak	452	5.24	516	4.8

Source: Economic Planning Unit, Malaysia

Note: RM = Ringgit Malaysia
HS = Household size

In Malaysia, relative poverty has been measured by using income disparity ratios of income groups (top 20 and bottom 40), ethnic groups and urban and rural dwellers. In addition, the Gini Coefficient and several other measures have also been used.

Objectives

The ultimate objective of public policy against poverty, as stated in the NEP, was to totally *eradicate* poverty. At the operational level, however, the more immediate objective has been to continuously *reduce* the incidence of poverty over set time periods. In line with this, the target during the NEP period has been to reduce the incidence of poverty in Peninsular Malaysia from 49.3 per cent in 1970 to 16.7 per cent in 1990[1]. Subsequently, under the NDP, a new target has been set, namely, to reduce the incidence of poverty to 7.2 per cent by the year 2000. In addition, it has also targeted the incidence of hardcore poverty to be reduced to 0.3 per cent by that year[2].

Another objective of the policy has been to reduce relative poverty or income inequality. In the NEP years, the focus has been on the reduction of the gaps among ethnic groups; rural and urban dwellers; and income groups. However, under the NDP, reducing intra-ethnic income gaps also became an objective. For all these objectives, no specific numerical targets have been set.

Strategies

To achieve the objective of poverty eradication, the primary strategies selected have been those that could provide opportunities to the poor to be involved or gain employment in higher-paying jobs or activities so that they could become self-supporting and increase their incomes to exceed the PLI. Less emphasis has been paid to welfare handouts as a means of dealing with poverty except for segments of the poor who have been unable to find gainful employment, such as the aged and handicapped.

In line with the above, the government has emphasised projects that enable the poor to modernise their traditional methods of production and participate in the mainstream of economic activities. In view that the majority of the poor were in the agricultural sector, the focus has been on providing them with the support and opportunities to be involved in modern farming and value-added processing of agricultural products as well as non-farm or off-farm activities or employment since they generally provide higher incomes than traditional farming. In this regard, a variety of innovative programmes have been implemented, such as :-

(a) the resettlement of the landless and those with uneconomic holdings in new land development schemes to work in and eventually own the rubber and oil palm plantations in the schemes. The settlers were also provided with single unit houses which came complete with piped water and electricity;

(b) the in-situ development of existing agricultural land through rehabilitation and consolidation of the land, the replanting of old commercial crops with new higher-yielding clones and better planting techniques. The land consolidation included a system of group farming wherein owners of small plots of adjacent land work them on a cooperative basis to reap the benefits of large scale operations;

(c) integrating agricultural and rural development with downstream processing of farm products and generally encouraging village industries and rural entrepreneurship in order to provide an additional source of income;

(d) double-cropping or off-season cropping, inter-cropping and mixed farming on the same plots of land to supplement main crop incomes;

(e)   the establishment of farmers' markets in urban centres to enable farmers to sell their products directly instead of through middlemen and thereby fetch better prices for them;

(f)   incorporating in most agricultural and rural development projects, a dose of training and education not only on topics pertaining to farming but also relating to work attitudes and values so as to motivate participants to be better, more productive farmers; and

(g)   a system of industrial and vocational training for rural manpower, including youths, as well as credit facilities and related support, to enable them to be employed in non-farm occupations or to start their own businesses not only in rural areas but also in urban centres.

Apart from income-generating projects, the government has also sought to improve the quality of life of the poor through the provision of infrastructural and social amenities as part of a broader programme to improve the quality of life of all Malaysians. For the rural population, they include the provision of potable and piped water, electricity, roads, medical and health services and schools, including rural hostels.

To deal specifically with hardcore poor households, a special programme for them was introduced in 1988. Known as the *Development Programme for the Hardcore Poor,* it involved the creation of a register and profile of hardcore poor households and the delivery of appropriate projects[3] to meet their specific needs such as additional opportunities to increase their employability and income, better housing, food supplements for children and educational assistance. In addition, since 1992, the major ethnic group among the hardcore poor, the *Bumiputera,* have been provided with interest-free loans to purchase shares in a unit trust scheme as another means towards increasing their income. By the end of 1995, about RM75.7 million in the form of dividends and bonuses has been paid to hardcore poor households who participated in the scheme.

In addition to the government, non-governmental organizations (NGOs)[4] and the private sector in Malaysia have also voluntarily involved themselves in helping to redress poverty, in recent years. Working in close cooperation with one another and complementing the government's efforts, they provide, *inter alia,* small business loans to the poor, industrial training and job opportunities, educational support for children of the poor and better housing. Among the NGOs, the *Amanah Ikhtiar Malaysia* (AIM) or Endeavour Trust of Malaysia has been the most successful. This is indicated by the fact that between 1991 and 1996 AIM provided interest-free

117

loans amounting to RM77 million to about 36,200 poor and hardcore poor households to enable them to venture into micro or small-scale businesses as well as poultry and livestock rearing. Most of these ventures were successful as reflected in the increased household income of the participants, almost all of whom were women, and the loan repayment rate of almost 100 per cent.

With regard to the planning, implementation and evaluation of poverty programmes, the functions have been allocated in the following manner:-

(a) The formulation of poverty reduction programmes in Malaysia has been led and coordinated by the Economic Planning Unit (EPU), Prime Minister's Department as an integral part of the process of formulating the nation's development plans. The process has been a multi-tiered one, involving village leaders at the bottom, the federal, state and local levels of the public service machinery (including the National Development Planning Committee which is chaired by the Chief Secretary to the Government), the Cabinet and, at the very top, Parliament. At the same time, it has also been broad-based, incorporating not only inputs from the parties mentioned above but also those of the universities, NGOs and individual experts. The main focus of the exercise has been on the achievements and shortcomings of existing programmes and the identification of remedial and new programs.

(b) The implementation of poverty programmes has been carried out by various Ministries through their operating agencies at the state and sub-state levels based on approved policies and programmes as well as supporting implementation guidelines. The task of coordinating and monitoring the implementation had been assigned originally to the Implementation Coordination Unit (ICU), Prime Minister's Department. To carry out this task, ICU has a multi-tiered set of multi-agency coordinating and monitoring committees. At the apex was the Working Committee for National Development which was chaired by the Chief Secretary to the Government, which in turn reported to the National Development Council, chaired by the Prime Minister. In 1995, as part of a bigger reorganization of ministerial functions, the ICU's function in this area was reassigned to the Ministry of Rural Development.

(c) The evaluation of the progress made in poverty reduction has been carried out mainly through periodic Household Income Surveys

118

conducted by the Department of Statistics which provided information on household income and the incidence of poverty. In addition, EPU and other agencies have also commissioned studies on more specific aspects of poverty as the need arose. The findings of these surveys and studies have then been used as inputs for the next round of the planning process.

Federal Government Development Expenditure for Poverty Reduction

In line with the policy emphasis on poverty reduction, about 28.3 or RM46.8 billion of Malaysia's consolidated development expenditure between 1971 and 1993 have been spent by the Federal government to finance poverty reduction programmes. In monetary terms, the amount spent has increased more than five-fold, from about RM2.4 billion during the Second Plan to RM13.9 billion in the Sixth Plan.

At the programme level, the expenditure has been distributed among programs to improve the productivity and income of the poor in the agricultural-rural sector and programs to improve their quality of life. As indicated by the expenditure breakdown for the Fifth and Sixth Plans shown in Table 3, a larger portion of the expenditure has been spent on agricultural programmes, all of which were essentially geared towards increasing productivity and income, reflecting the strategic emphasis given to them.

Achievements

As a result of the efforts taken to reduce poverty, the incidence of poverty[5] has been reduced from between 50 to 60 per cent[6] in 1970 to 8.9 per cent in 1995. More specifically, the incidence of poverty in rural areas has been reduced to 15.3 per cent and that in urban areas, to 3.7 per cent. With regard to hardcore poverty, as a result of the implementation of the Development Programme for the Hardcore Poor during the 1991-95 period, its overall incidence has been reduced from 4.0 per cent in 1990 to 2.1 per cent in 1995 while that for urban and rural areas were reduced from 1.4 to 0.8 per cent and from 5.2 to 3.7 per cent, respectively (Table 7.4).

119

Table 7.3 Malaysia: Federal Government Development Expenditure for Poverty Reduction, Fifth and Sixth Malaysia Plans (RM million)

Programme	Fifth Malaysia Plan, 1986-90	%	Sixth Malaysia Plan, 1991-95	%
Agriculture	**7,127.0**	**54.9**	**8,058.8**	**58.0**
New land development	2,117.5		1,184.0	
Regional development	657.1		930.5	
Integrated Agricultural Development Project (IADP)	1,021.8		1,351.4	
Drainage and irrigation	200.3		844.6	
Replanting	581.2		935.8	
Rehabilitation	812.7		732.4	
Padi fertilizer subsidy	396.8		402.0	
Agricultural credit, processing and marketing	586.1		507.0	
Extension and other services	28.9		373.5	
Fisheries	264.4		370.0	
Livestock	130.9		191.4	
Other agricultural programmes	329.3		236.2	
Industry	**77.0**	**0.6**	**118.9**	**0.9**
Village/small industry	77.0		118.9	
Infrastructure	**3,434.4**	**26.5**	**1,793.2**	**12.9**
Rural roads	1,161.4		1,085.0	
Rural electricity	569.6		355.1	
Rural water supply	1,703.4		353.1	
Social	**2,332.3**	**18.0**	**3,929.9**	**28.3**
Rural health service	181.0		123.2	
Rural primary and secondary schools	1,621.7		3,094.1	
Community development	32.0		162.0	
Applied food and nutrition programme	10.0		16.2	
Low-cost housing	345.0		228.0	
Regrouping of traditional villages	24.0		49.0	
Village rehabilitation programme	51.0		93.0	
Squatters resettlement and control	13.9		15.1	
NADI programme	3.4		3.7	
Welfare	4.0		53.9	
Programmes for Orang Asli (Aborigines)	46.3		91.8	
Total	**12,970.7**	**100.0**	**13,900.8**	**100.0**

Source: Economic Planning Unit, Malaysia

Table 7.4   Malaysia: Incidence of Poverty and Hardcore Poverty 1970, 1985, 1990, 1995 (%)

	1970[1]	1985	1990	1995
Poverty	49.3	20.7	16.3 (17.1)	8.9 (9.6)
Urban	21.3	8.5	7.1 (7.5)	1.7 (4.1)
Rural	58.7	27.3	21.1 (21.8)	15.3 (16.1)
Hardcore Poverty	-	6.9	3.9 (4.0)	2.1 (2.2)
Urban	-	2.4	1.3 (1.4)	0.8 (0.9)
Rural	-	9.3	5.2 (5.2)	3.7 (3.7)

Source: Economic Planning Unit, Malaysia

Notes: 1   Figures refer to Peninsular Malaysia only.
2   Figures in brackets refer to incidence of poverty if non-citizens are included. Figures on the incidence of poverty among Malaysian citizen and non-citizens began to be collected from 1990 only.

In addition, there are positive indications to show that the various programmes aimed at improving the quality of life of the poor in rural areas have been successful. By the end of 1995, about 88 per cent of the urban and 72 per cent of rural poor households in Malaysia had access to electricity. In addition, 92 per cent of the urban poor and 65 per cent of the rural poor households had access to safe drinking water. In terms of accessibility to health facilities, about 88 per cent of the poor in urban areas and 77 per cent in the rural areas were within nine kilometres of either a Government or private clinic. Rural areas were also served by mobile dental teams and dispensaries, village health teams and the flying doctor service to remote and outlying areas. Furthermore, about 94 per cent of rural poor households and almost all the urban poor were within nine kilometres of a primary school, while about 60 per cent in rural and 96 per cent in urban areas were within the same distance of a secondary school. In addition, various kinds of educational assistance such as scholarships and free textbooks, food and accommodation, and uniforms were provided to students in poor households.

With regard to the distribution of the benefits of growth, the available data indicate that there has been an increasingly fairer distribution of income among the various income groups. The Gini Coefficient decreased from 0.513 in 1970 to about 0.464 in 1995. In line with this, among income groups the share of the bottom 40 per cent of households of total household income increased from 11.5 to 13.4 per cent over the same period.

Future Challenges

It is envisaged that on the poverty front there will be at least three major challenges to be overcome in the years ahead. They are:-

(a) *Ensuring that the economy continues to expand and that price stability is maintained.* The expanding economy is needed to provide continuing employment opportunities for poor households and improve their income. Price stability is necessary to ensure that income gains are not negated by price increases, particularly of items that comprise the CPI basket of goods.

(b) *Reducing further the incidence of poverty and hardcore poverty once they have reached single digit figures.* It is expected that once the incidence of poverty has reached single digit figures, the task of reducing it further will be more difficult and probably more costly, too. The fact that the incidence of hardcore poverty could only be reduced by one per cent over the four years period between 1990 and 1993 (from four to three per cent) is an indication of this. The difficulty will be greater because those who comprise the remnant group will be people who have not been able, for various reasons, to take advantage of the opportunities provided by government programmes and Malaysia's ever expanding economy, to better themselves.

(c) *Reducing income inequalities and relative poverty.* In essence, this will require a faster income growth on a prolonged basis for the poor and lower income groups than that for the top income group. Achieving this in the context of an increasingly liberal economic environment will be particularly challenging. Fiscal policies, including progressive income tax, can help by reducing (disposable) income gaps. However, they may also have disincentive effects on further

122

business expansion or income generation by people in the top income group.

Some possible lessons from the Malaysian experience

As evident from the preceding description and analysis, Malaysia has had a long and successful experience in reducing poverty and generally in bringing about rapid socio-economic development. The experience is probably unique to Malaysia. Nevertheless, its broad features and underlying principles and strategies are probably relevant to other developing countries as well. There are at least 10 of them, namely:-

(a) Peaceful co-existence among ethnic or other groups in society as well as close cooperation among ethnic-based political parties are crucial if there is to be political stability and for socio-economic development to proceed unhindered by strife among them.

(b) The inherent tendency of a plural society to disintegrate or at least compartmentalise itself into competing or hostile sub-groups can be countered and contained through a multiple-pronged, coordinated and persistent attack on it.

(c) Governments must genuinely be people-based and ensure that there is broad-participation in policy making so that public policies are based on a national consensus, truly address the peoples needs and, therefore, are supported and have a better chance of succeeding.

(d) A critical component of poverty reduction efforts is continuous and rapid growth to enable the poor, amongst others, to increase their incomes.

(e) Pure economic growth alone cannot guarantee social harmony, particularly in a plural society. It must be balanced by a strong and real emphasis on equitable distribution of development benefits. Governments have to ensure that this takes place.

(f) For greater impact, Government interventions and programmes to reduce poverty must be a properly coordinated multi-agency and multi-pronged effort.

(g) The multi-pronged effort should focus on productivity-increasing and income-generating programme. Here, a major solution or prerequisite

123

to a solution is education and training for the poor and, so that there is no intergenerational transfer of poverty to their children. At the same time, however, attention should also be paid to improving the quality of life of the poor through upgrading or expansions of public services, social amenities and physical infrastructure. Welfare assistance or handouts should be limited to special cases to avoid the embedding of the dole mentality among the poor.

(h) The poor are not one homogenous group. There are many sub-groups of the poor such as the hardcore poor, women or female-headed families, old people, the handicapped and indigenous communities. Each of these sub-groups typically have unique problems and, therefore, have to be dealt with differently if the problems are to be overcome.

(i) Public policies or programmes must not only be relevant but also innovative and flexible to enable them to be more effective in overcoming social problems, which are typically complex and dynamic. The special unit trust scheme for the hardcore poor in Malaysia is an example of such a programme.

(j) NGOs and the private sector can and should be encouraged to make their contributions towards the minimization of social problems, including the reduction of poverty, and not be regarded as competitors of government agencies.

Appendix 1

Table 7.A.1 Malaysia: Projects under the development programme for the hardcore poor

Objective	Project	Department/Agency
Increase the quality of life	Construction of new houses, renovation of existing houses, flush toilets, electricity and water supply, community halls, roads, drainage, mosques.	District Office, Department of Public Health, Department of Water Supply, National Energy Corporation, Local Governments.
Increase income	Village industries, cash crops, rearing of poultry, cattle, sheep, goats and ducks, aquaculture, low interest or interest-free credit, marketing facilities, land development, fishing equipment.	District Office, Veterinary Department, Department of Agriculture, Department of Fisheries, Malaysian Fishery Development Authority, Rubber Industry Smallholders Development Authority, Agriculture Bank, Federal Agricultural Marketing Authority, *Amanah Ikhtiar Malaysia* (NGO).
Human resource development	Study tours, special training for farm families, skill training, rural technology workshops, community library, rural hostels, leadership and motivation training, training in marketing.	Department of Agriculture, Veterinary Department, Department of Youth and Sports, Community Development Division of the Ministry of Rural Development, Department of Fisheries, Federal Agricultural Marketing Authority, District Office, *Yayasan Basmi Kemiskinan* (NGO).
Health and nutrition	Food supplement and subsidised milk for primary school children, food basket for malnourished pre-schoolers, school health education.	Department of Public Health, Community Development Division of the Ministry of Rural Development, Ministry of Education.
Direct assistance	Old Folks' Home (Without Kin), allowance for handicapped workers, financial assistance for the aged, scholarships, loan on text books, not interest loans to purchase shares in a unit trust scheme.	Social Welfare Department, Department of Youth and Sports, Ministry of Education, National Equity Corporation.

Source: Implementation Coordination Unit, Malaysia

Appendix 2

Table 7.A.2 Malaysia: Involvement of NGO in poverty reduction programmes

NGO	Activity	Funding Source
1. *Amanah Ikhtiar Malaysia (NGO)* (Endeavour Trust of Malaysia)	Credit facility	Private sector contributions and partial Government assistance
2. *Yayasan Basmi Kemiskinan Selangor* (Selangor Poverty Eradication Foundation)	Housing, education, training, small economic projects.	Private sector contributions and partial Government assistance
3. *Yayasan Kemiskinan Kelantan* (Kelantan Poverty Eradication Foundation)	Education	Government contribution
4. *Yayasan Pahang* (Pahang Foundation)	Education	Self-financing
5. *Yayasan Terengganu* (Terengganu Foundation)	Education	Self-financing

Source: Implementation Coordination Unit, Malaysia.

Notes

1. No numerical targets were set for the states of Sabah and Sarawak since there were no reliable figures on poverty incidence in those states in 1970.
2. This target was subsequently readjusted to 0.5 per cent during the preparation of the Seventh Malaysia Plan, 1996-2000.
3. Please see Appendix 1 for details.
4. Please see Appendix 2 for details.

5. The incidence of poverty is derived by dividing the number of poor households with the total number of households.
6. This is an estimate based on the 1970 incidence of poverty in Peninsular Malaysia (49.3 per cent) and the 1976 incidence of poverty in Sabah (58.3 per cent) and Sarawak (56.5 per cent).

8 "Practise What You Preach': Is Participant Empowerment Desirable in Micro-Development NGOs?

JANE OLIVER

Introduction

According to the OECD, private and official sources of financing of non-governmental organizations (NGOs) worldwide increased by two-fold between 1970 and 1988 (Clark, 1991, p. 46). At the national level, for example in India, there was a two-fold increase in foreign aid, and a thirty-fold increase in government funding of NGOs between 1986 and 1990 (Robinson, 1991, p. 33). Some 15,000-20,000 NGOs are engaged actively in rural development in India, attempting to alleviate rural poverty in a variety of ways.

As the numbers of NGOs and volume of funds being channelled to them increase worldwide, questions of accountability arise as NGO observers ask in whose interests NGOs work - their donors, government, 'beneficiaries', Board of Trustees, staff, etc. Concern for NGOs accountability has led to the prescription in NGO literature that NGOs should evaluate how democratically they operate as organizations. This issue is best understood using a political analysis framework of organizations. Questions need to be asked, like what form of organizational democracy are NGO observers implying? Do NGO workers themselves, desire to operate democratically, and how? Finally, do NGOs believe democratic organization is worthwhile and feasible, or is it yet another unobtainable claim others have made for NGOs?

This paper explores first, claims made by and about NGOs in the literature - claims about their structure, claims about their function, and then the implied linkage of these two sets of claims to the issue of organizational democracy. Second, the paper clarifies the concept of organizational democracy with particular reference to participatory democratic forms, at both an analytical and experiential level. Third, the paper explores generally and specifically whether or not NGO workers themselves have expressed a desire to operate democratically. Finally, the paper concludes by pointing to a number of issues subsequent papers should address, such as the feasibility of organizational democracy within the NGO sector.

'NGO-lore'

Referring to a range of 'voluntary' organizations involved in rural development work using the single all-inclusive term, 'NGO', is notoriously problematic. Nevertheless, I will use this umbrella term to refer to the whole gamut of voluntary organizations which belong primarily in the 'associational' world, distinct from but often overlapping with the 'bureaucratic' (government and business) and 'personal' worlds (Billis, 1989, p. 11). Thus I recognize that different NGOs, depending, fundamentally, on which world they overlap most with, will operate on somewhat different organizing principles. When I refer to those NGOs engaged specifically in 'micro-development' - development activities at a community or village scale of social organization (Fowler, 1988, p. 26), I differentiate between two types of NGO: 'membership support organizations' (MSOs - staffed and elected by its members), and 'grassroots support organizations' (GSOs - staffed largely by professionals, and supporting MSOs), (Carroll, 1992). Clearly, organizational democracy implies different things for these different types of organization.

There is a confusing mixture of claims about NGOs all of which seem to be tangled into one mess, which I do not profess to untangle here. There are those made by NGO practitioners, those made by NGO analysts (academic researchers, donor agencies, governments), and those made by NGO analysts as an interpretation of NGO practitioners' claims, though this differentiation is often difficult to tease out.

To start with, NGOs have made many claims about their strengths in particular, over the last 15-20 years, some claims of which have been tested recently and others of which have become 'NGO -lore' (Farrington and Bebbington, 1993, p. 100). One key claim is that NGOs are more effective than government in micro-development (Farrington and Bebbington, 1993; Fowler, 1988). Their effectiveness is claimed to be due largely to their organizational distinctiveness, that both their societal functions and organizational structures are suggested to be of a democratic nature. However, few analysts have done 'institutional ethnographies' of NGOs to back up NGOs claims (Farrington and Bebbington, 1993, p. 56). They prefer instead to evaluate project performance in the field (Fowler, 1988, p. 6).

Furthermore, organizations generally are usually thought to be 'rational enterprises in which their members seek common goals [which] tends to discourage discussion or attribution of political motive' (Morgan, 1986, p. 142). This preferred goal-oriented analytical approach to organizations in general and NGOs in particular, partly reflects NGO staff's stronger feelings of commitment to their work of transforming society at large, rather than to a concern with examining the organization itself (Clark, 1991, p. 62). Nevertheless, NGO analysts have focused on two sets of organizational claims made by NGOs and analysts, about the societal function and internal organizational structure of NGOs. Furthermore, analysts are only beginning to imply the linkage between these two sets of claims, suggesting the need for a political analysis of NGOs.

The first set of claims is to do with the societal function of NGOs. NGO analysts have tried to categorize NGOs, where they make up an entirely new sector - 'third sector' or 'voluntary sector' - differentiated from the public (state) or private (business) sectors on the basis of their function (Esman and Uphoff, 1984, p. 18). The first or public sector performs the functions of 'command and control', while the second or private sector sets out to make a profit (Bratton, 1989). NGOs, though performing altruistic acts like governments, operate instead on the principle of voluntarism (Fowler, 1988). They are value-driven, and are on a 'social change mission' (Farrington and Bebbington, 1993; Clark, 1991; Brown and Covey, 1989). Of particular relevance is that some NGOs set themselves the explicit function or goal of empowering people, that is, helping them to change their political, social and economic situation (Edwards and Hulme, 1992; Bratton, 1989). This is related to the further claim that GOs have the function of democratizing society and strengthening civil society (Farrington and Bebbington, 1993; Clark, 1991; Bratton, 1989; Korten, 1987).

The second set of claims is to do with the organizational structure of NGOs. These claims lie at the root of the current debates on 'comparative advantage', and 'scaling-up'. NGOs are believed to have several advantages, compared to government, like being more flexible and responsive to local people (Clark, 1991; Fowler, 1988). They lie primarily in the 'associational' rather than the 'bureaucratic, world, and therefore are more likely to be democratic than hierarchical (Billis and MacKeith, 1992).

They hold autocratic forms of leadership in disdain (Clark, 1991). Therefore, analysts believe that organizational growth, as a scaling-up strategy, will make NGOs increasingly more formalized and bureaucratic. This structural organizational change will create new management lines. The distance between staff and key decision makers will increase and consequently damage the NGO's original advantages of adaptability and responsiveness (Billis and MacKeith, 1992, p. 124). A second scaling-up strategy of collaboration with government, has led some NGOs to worry about the 'loss of institutional autonomy and independence'. This is especially so if NGOs and governments form structural (rather than operational) linkages (Farrington and Bebbington, 1993, p. 174). Overall, this set of claims emphasizes that NGO analysts are increasingly concerned with the 'good governance' and 'internal democracy' of NGOs (Farrington and Bebbington, 1993).

What is intriguing is that some NGO workers and analysts have linked these two sets of organizational claims. Are NGOs interested in 'practising what they preach' (Billis and MacKeith, 1992, p. 120)? In other words, 'while NGOs may be seen by some as vehicles of democratization, their own house is not always in order in this regard' (Farrington and Bebbington, 1993, p. 24). As one policy analyst working with Proshika MUK (an NGO) in Bangladesh observes, 'It has sufficed till recently for NGOs to talk about democratization and the widening of franchise, of empowerment, while neglecting to apply these noble principles themselves' (Hannan, 1995, p. 9).

The structure-function linkage within an NGO means that it is important to consider whether or not the NGO matches its democratic societal function to an internally democratic organizational structure. Observation of this linkage has emerged partly from a recognition of the mismatch between the nature of micro-development and governments' structures. Micro-development takes place in an uncertain and complex environment that requires responses which are locally responsive and flexible, not centralized and rigid (Rondinelli, 1990; Bratton, 1989; Fowler, 1988). By examining the nature of micro-development, it is clear that certain organizational structures are better suited to carrying out the task than others (Fowler, 1988, p. 7). This is not to take a determinist view of organizational function and structure, for adopting a 'social actor analysis' of NGOs means individuals within NGOs do have room to manoeuvre (Farrington and Bebbington, 1993, p. 45).

This structure-function linkage has been made further within discussion of the issue of 'accountability', currently being emphasized within NGO analysis (Edwards and Hulme, 1994, p. 21). NGOs operate in an environment made up of multiple constituencies, where they are accountable to any number of actors - donors, governments, project partners, Board of Trustees, clients, staff, public, media (Clark, 1993, p. 73; Brown and Covey, 1989, p. 28). Often, it appears that NGOs are more accountable to their donors and governments, that is, their paymasters, and less so to their clients and staff. Therefore, NGOs' (especially GSOs) claim to represent the poor is questionable because they often are not formally accountable to nor composed of the poor (Farrington and Bebbington, 1993, p. 111). In other words, while an NGO may espouse the goal or function of democratizing rural society, the organization itself is not structured democratically, allowing neither representation of the poor nor their decision making contribution to the goals the organization is working towards. There lies the gap between rhetoric and practice.

But what exactly does an internally democratic organization look like? What organizations have practised organizational democracy? How comparable to NGOs are others' experiences with it? Do different types of NGOs operate on different principles of democracy?

What is organizational democracy?

Definition

Consideration of the issue of organizational democracy makes explicit an understanding of organizations as political systems, specifically as systems of government. 'Organizations, like governments, employ some system of "rule" as a means of creating and maintaining order among their members' (Morgan, 1986, p. 145). Thus organizations may rule in an autocratic (absolute rule exercized through use of personal privilege by individual or small group), bureaucratic (rule of law exercized through use of written word), technocratic (rule of law exercized through knowledge and expert power, i.e. by scientists and engineers), or democratic (rule exercized through power of populace; different forms - representative, participatory, or codetermined by opposing parties) way, or any combination of these. Each type of rule is political but just of a different kind, which draws on different principles of legitimacy (ibid., pp. 145-46).

Organizational democracy encompasses different forms of democracy like co-determination, representative democracy and direct or participatory democracy. I explore here the latter form of democracy, for it develops the notion of 'self-management' or 'empowerment of beneficiaries' (*sic* 'members') which I expand in the next section on the relevance of this concept to NGOs. I refer primarily to literature on cooperatives because it deals primarily with the practice of participatory democracy. I recognize however that there is much recent experience of representative forms of organizational 'rule' found in corporate management literature.

Rothschild-Whitt and Lindenfeld (1982), drawing on a tradition of participatory (direct) democracy as it refers to a work environment, refer to 'workplace democracy', which they define as follows:

> Democratic workplaces are united in their attempt to break down the division between management and labour, planners and workers, so that all who do the work of the organization have an equal voice in its management and a fair share of the fruits of their labour. What they are seeking to alter, then is nothing short of the structure of power in organizations. The aim is not the simple *transference* of power from one official to another; it is the *abolition* of the pyramid *in toto*. It is an attempt to accomplish organizational tasks cooperatively and democratically, without recourse to hierarchical authority structures or the stratification systems that accompany them (ibid., p. 6).

Bernstein (1982) argues that this conception of workplace democracy counters, first, Weber's strict authoritarian structure of an ideal, monocratic type of bureaucratic administration, and; second, F.W. Taylor's principles of scientific management, where jobs were segmented and specialized, and the labour process was divided into intellectual and manual tasks. Instead, workplace democracy promotes the idea that there is no division between management and labour, rather that control over the entire labour process rests in the hands of members-employees-owners (Rothschild and Whitt, 1986, p. 2).

Rothschild-Whitt and Lindenfeld (1982, pp. 1-4), drawing on their research on American cooperatives, differentiate between two types of democratic organizations, on the basis of size. There are small grassroots worker-collectives, and large democratically managed organizations. The worker-collectives typically have 12-20 members. The group is small enough such that all major decisions are made by the entire group in plenary meetings. Work roles are holistic, embracing both administrative and performance tasks. Internal education is stressed, so that specialized knowledge is demystified, by workers sharing tasks, and rotating jobs. Most of these American and European worker-collectives originated in the counter-culture movement of the 1960s. Almost all developed since 1970. They encompass almost every domain of social life but especially in the service sector as health collectives, free schools, food cooperatives, etc. In the USA these collective organizations constitute the largest category of contemporary democratic workplaces.

The latter democratically managed organizations have up to several hundred workers, and in some cases, thousands. Therefore, there is usually some job specialization, but this is combined with the goal of internal education. Workers share their knowledge as much as possible with other workers, again through task sharing and job rotation but possibly not as frequently as in the smaller worker-collectives. Some stratification exists, where positions have differential importance and are rewarded unequally. However, as in the smaller collectives, the income ratio between the highest and lowest paid workers is 2:1 or 3:1. This compares with many American corporations who typically have a 100:1 income ratio. In both the small collectives and large democratic organizations, authority may be delegated but the entire membership can recall that authority or retain the final say in a dispute. Examples of the latter organization are the Mondragon worker production cooperatives in the Basque region of Spain, Israeli Kibbutzim, and earlier Yugoslavian workers' councils.

'Intellectual roots'

Perhaps the two most important 'intellectual roots' of this form of organizational democracy are participatory democratic theory and anarchism. One of the earliest modern writers on participatory democracy, who reinterpreted the work of those theorists from the turn of the century, Rousseau, J.S. Mill, G.D.H. Cole, believes that decision making participation has several benefits, but most of all a psychological, educative effect (Pateman, 1970). Participation must begin at a local level so that individuals make decisions which directly concern their lives. Political decision making is located not only in the sphere of government but also within the workplace. A participatory workplace is one in which there is no hierarchy of superior-subordinate relationships between workers. All workers learn to share power and take responsibility for the work process. They develop a sense of interdependence or community as they participate collectively in the governance of the workplace. They therefore develop a 'democratic character', and learn democratic procedures. They are then ready to transfer these attitudes and skills to the wider society. Thus a democratic workplace acts as a model for a democratic society (Pateman, 1970, p. 31).

Anarchism introduces the idea that the most durable forms of organizations are those voluntary associations of people who spontaneously come together out of a common need. External authority is unnecessary because people inherently are self-disciplined and independent, and therefore able to become self-organized. Yet people are also interdependent and therefore benefit from acts of 'mutual aid'.

The key anarchist contribution to the nature of collective organization is the unity of means and ends:

> Anarchist strategies stress the congruence of means and ends, and thus, for example, would not propose mandatory organizations to re-educate people for a free society. They would not advocate violent means to achieve a peaceful society; nor would they choose centralized means to attain a decentralized society (Rothschild and Whitt, 1986, p. 17).

This may be termed a 'politics of function' (Dennison, 1972), or strategy of means-end match, whereby 'an organization is political if, in its very form, it exemplifies the sort of democratically run, community-based organization that could provide a model for a new society' (Rothschild-Whitt and Lindenfeld, 1982, p. 17). Thus a democratic society can develop only out of democratic organizations operating within society.

Consensus decision making

A crucial identifying characteristic of collective-democratic organization is collective, not individual authority (Rothschild and Whitt, 1986, p. 2). Indeed, it does not imply any authority structure - leaders may be rotated or indeed not even required (Rothschild and Whitt, 1986, p. 52). Decisions are made by consensus. It is a process in which the entire membership of a cooperative collectively formulates the agenda, and negotiates decisions. The agenda of decisions includes all major policy decisions of the organization, like hiring and firing, salaries, division of labour, etc. Members discuss the issue until all agree. No decision is binding or legitimate unless the entire collective is engaged in the decision (ibid., pp. 51-52). The process of making decisions is almost more important than the actual decision made. The means rather than the end counts for more:

> It reveals that the group is not concerned with simple efficiency as it is with exemplifying in its internal process the values of self-

expression and group cohesion ... it reflects, and perhaps serves to instill, cooperation and self-determination, attributes these groups usually want to foster (ibid., p. 52).

Pateman (1970) argues that two important effects arise from collective decision making. First, individuals are more likely to accept decisions which are made collectively. Second, there is an 'integrative' effect, for collectively participating in decisions causes the individual to experience a greater feeling of identity with and belonging to a larger community.

Of course, the oft-cited argument against consensus decision making is its lengthy nature. Yet proponents of hierarchical decision making, characteristic of bureaucratic organizations, fail to consider the counter argument, that decisions made in bureaucracies are often halted or skewed in their implementation by subordinates who resent their superiors not consulting them for their opinions.

From the foregoing, workplace (direct) democracy appears to be more than just a question of accountability between an organization and its various constituents. It is a fundamentally different conception of the meaning of authority, and how that authority is maintained and/or challenged. And it is about making the work process a holistic activity where various tasks are shared and jobs are rotated, such that no hierarchy, therefore inequality, develops between administrative and manual tasks. Through these two organizational changes, the entire membership of the organization enjoys access to a wider scope of information from which to make decisions. Each worker is better able to engage more fully in setting the organization's agenda, and making decisions on the organization's activities, from the mundane to the complex.

But how relevant are collectives' experiences with organizational democracy to NGOs? Which type of NGO desires to practise which form of organizational democracy?

How is organizational democracy relevant to NGOs?

Collectives and NGOs compared While producer or consumer collectives do not appear immediately to be relevant to Indian NGOs, for example, there are a few commonalities between them that raise some important issues about the nature of organization.

Rothschild and Whitt (1986) make at least four points about collectives that strike a chord with NGOs. First, collectives tend to originate from, and continue to identify with, social movements. These authors therefore have

136

referred to collectives as 'social movement organizations'. Second, their goals tend to be oriented toward making personal and social changes through their actions. Third, they developed parallel to mainstream organizations which were oriented toward fulfilling social needs. Fourth, workplaces, be they collectives or NGOs, perform an educational function for their staff.

To elaborate: first, the growth in both collectives and NGOs has tended to follow social movements. American collectives formed in at least five distinct waves following major movements for social change. Those which formed in four waves between 1840 and 1930 arose out of workers' protests to increased mechanization and standardization in industry. Those that formed beginning in 1970 followed the civil rights, antiwar, women's, students' and environmental movements of the 1960s (Rothschild and Whitt, 1986, p. 10).

In the case of NGOs, there is the Indian example. Indian voluntary organizations developed in spirit if not in form from at least four different movements occurring at different stages of Indian history. There was the Social Reform Movement in the early 1800s, *Swadeshi* cum Gandhian Movement of the early 1900s, student *Naxalite* Movement in the mid-1960s to mid-1970s, and J.P. Movement around the time of Emergency in the mid to late 1970s. The latter three movements in particular formed the basis for voluntary work and development of voluntary organizations in several parts of India (PRIA, 1991, pp. 23-32).

According to Rothschild and Whitt (1986), the effect of an organization having a social movement orientation is that the organization is less likely to have its goals displaced or coopted. The organization constantly gains inspiration, guidance and moral support from the spirit of the movement and other organizations connected to the movement. Whereas if the organization is not connected to the social-historical purpose of a wider movement, the organization becomes more bounded, is likely to exist for its own sake, and therefore allows displacement or cooptation of its original social change goals (ibid., p. 140). So for example, NGOs in India, like *Gramin Vikas Vigyan Samiti* in Rajasthan, and *Banvasi Seva Ashram* in Uttar Pradesh, have Founders who were involved in the Gandhian and J.P. movements. They continue to meet with other Gandhians and organizations inspired by these movements, supporting each other in their current work. Consequently, they have retained remarkably similar goals to those that Gandhi espoused some fifty years ago, like removal of untouchability.

Second, both collectives and NGOs are claimed to be value oriented and engaged in a process of social change. While collectives have formed generally out of their members' value and ideologically driven desire to structure themselves in a collective-democratic manner, so many NGOs have formed out of their Founders' value and ideologically driven desire to promote social changes in the wider society. In both cases, a different type of motivation, other than just monetary rewards, career advancement, and improving the effectiveness and efficiency of the organization's performance, drives members or workers to do their work. Clark (1991) refers therefore to the high staff commitment found in NGOs (ibid., p. 61).

Brown and Covey (1989) prefer to call NGOs 'social change organizations (SCOs)', thereby making explicit their value laden societal goals. They characterize SCOs as having a 'social change mission', where they 'emphasize the creation of better (more equitable, more innovative, more productive, more healthy) communities and societies':

> They articulate and work for visions of a better world. Social change missions commit SCOs to changing their environments (ibid., p. 28).

An NGO may aim to promote improved gender relations, or environmental sustainability, or economic and social justice. Social change organizations or NGOs focus their attention on some aspect of society that they see is problematic, and then set out to change it, firmly convinced that they have the duty, if not right, and ability to make changes.

NGOs, like collectives, therefore tend to attract workers or members who themselves hold a particular set of values:

> Visions of change and development are central to SCOs. These visionary missions make values and ideologies central features of SCO life. Members of SCOs are motivated by shared social values, and they often justify the organization's activities in terms of such values. Ideologies underpin action by explaining linkages among what exists, what should be, and how changes can be accomplished (ibid., p. 28).

It is this moralizing, value orientation of workers in both collectives and NGOs that leads to the expectation that a means-end or structure-function match should operate. Otherwise, there exists a credibility gap between what a worker says and what s/he does. The personal becomes (publicly) political.

Third, both collectives and NGOs operate parallel to established institutions. A health collective offers an alternative to a city hospital, a food cooperative is instead of Safeway, etc. In the case of NGOs, they offer opportunities for social change as an alternative to what government offers. NGOs, like collectives, are attempting to fulfil people's social needs that for whatever reason are not being met by the established institutions. In both cases, collectives and NGOs try either to offer their own organization as a model, or to create a model for a new type of society they envision, based on an explicit set of values. And they believe they can do so because they are a different type of organization, in both function and structure.

A fourth point of comparison is the scope for education about democratic attitudes and skills through decision making participation within a workplace. What is interesting for micro-development NGOs is that those workers who originate from villages within the NGO's vicinity of operation may learn new democratic attitudes and skills if they work for a collective-democratic NGO. One might expect that the worker would bring a deeper understanding to the meaning of democratic participation which her/his NGO espouses, if s/he practises the same in the internal operations of the NGO itself. That is, the NGO exists as a model for the changes it expects the wider society to make.

Nevertheless, these points of comparison are very general and do not deal with the nature of specific types of NGOs, whose differences partly are based on the different roles that participants in the organization play. MSOs appear to be the type of NGO which could most easily operate like a collective, practising a participatory or direct form of democracy. Workers are members, that is those who decide about and do development work are also the ones who benefit from development projects.

GSOs, on the other hand, are second tier NGOs whose workers are either representatives of the MSOs of which they are members, or whose workers are not members of MSOs but who still represent the interests of MSOs. In this case, it appears a representative form of democracy has the potential to operate in this type of NGO.

However, it is not just a case of what role the participant plays in the organization which determines what form of democracy could operate. There are certain conditions that facilitate formation of collectivist-democratic organizations, in general (Rothschild and Whitt, 1986). I will mention only one condition which is of particular relevance to the circumstances of NGOs, as full analysis of a number of conditions would constitute a separate paper on the 'feasibility' of NGOs practising workplace democracy.

One condition is that a collectivist-democratic organization does not depend substantially on an external financial support base. Doing so, will lower the participation of and responsiveness to members. Yet, NGOs of all shapes and sizes, by nature of belonging to the voluntary sector, depend up to one hundred per cent on outside grants from donor agencies and/or governments, and donations, for their day-to-day operations. Unlike producer or consumer cooperatives, they are not primarily self supporting. This generally high external resource dependence has consequences for the decision making structure of all kinds of NGOs, MSOs included. Financiers may have a much stronger say about how the NGO should operate than the NGOs' actual workers and/or 'beneficiaries'/members.

NGO evidence of desire While I have offered points of comparison between these organizational types, what evidence exists that NGO workers themselves are aware of and desire to create directly democratic organizations? Do the organization's workers reflect these society focused democratic goals back onto themselves and their own organizational work structures and processes? Is the personal political for them, as it appears to be for workers in collectives?

The first piece of evidence actually emerges not from MSOs or GSOs, but rather from large British NGOs. Billis and MacKeith (1992), in a study of organizational and management challenges confronting larger voluntary organizations operating in the UK, found that 'one of the most frequently mentioned challenges was the conflict between staff and senior managers concerning the process by which decisions were made in the organization' (ibid., p. 119). While the senior managers believed they should operate in a hierarchy of authority, the 'subordinate staff' felt they should work in a democratic manner. Their rationale for this expectation was based on the:

> agencies' self-proclaimed approach to development - an approach in which beneficiaries are seen as equal partners participating fully in the running of their projects. The argument of the subordinate staff was that the agencies should practise what they preached (ibid., p. 120).

Hodson (1992), a previous Chief Executive of ACTIONAID, confirms this view: 'In believing that the world can and should be more egalitarian and democratic, NGO employees want to see these characteristics functioning in their own organization' (Hodson, 1992, p. 129).

That is, workers in some northern based NGOs appear to have the same concern with matching their societal and organizational values, as do collectives. But what of southern based NGOs, for example, in India?

The Society for Participatory Research in Asia (PRIA) is one such organization, or GSO, that articulates a concern with consistency between societal goals and organizational practice. It is an NGO itself which offers the service, to field based NGOs, of acting as a facilitator for the threefold evaluation of: programmes; the organization itself; and the perspective or vision of the NGO. Their philosophy is that the workers of the NGO in question, other GSOs, are interested in improving their work and capable of evaluating themselves and their work, that evaluation is an 'educational experience as opposed to a regulating mechanism' (PRIA, 1992, p. 10). In which case, PRIA facilitates every stage of the evaluation in direct consultation with the NGO's workers:

> It is our view that Participatory Evaluation methodology is consistent with participatory models of development which are now being experimented with at grass-roots level throughout the world... Given this thrust of people-centred, bottom-up development, it makes consistent sense to ensure that the process of reflection and evaluation has similar characteristics and meaning. It will be a contradiction to have a people-centred, bottom-up process of development evaluated through commissioned agents appointed by resource-providers (ibid., p. 11).

Representatives of at least ten Indian NGOs (GSOs) participated in an international workshop on participatory evaluation PRIA organized in 1988 (PRIA, 1988, p. 81). PRIA has facilitated participatory evaluations of at least nine Indian GSOs, illustrating that these NGOs perceive the value logic of matching their societal work with their organizational practice. Their democratic societal goals are reflected in their attempt to practise democratic internal dynamics. More generally, PRIA's practice of participatory evaluation is just one aspect of a larger movement in participatory action research and action research that has roots in India, the UK, Australia, and Canada. This movement is based firmly on the belief that values must be matched by practices.

Though I have provided only three examples, all the evidence is yet to come in about NGOs, of all types, awareness and experience of organizational democracy.

Conclusions

Further research is required to address a number of questions suggested in this discussion. One question is, how feasible is organizational democracy in the NGO sector? Specifically, what form of organizational democracy is most feasible for what type of NGO, considering they differ in size, the roles their participants play, the number and type of constituencies to whom they are accountable, and the extent of their external financial dependence? Rothschild and Whitt (1986) emphasize that workplace democracy is both conditional, and subject to constraints. I will elaborate briefly two aspects.

First, the environment must be considered. As Farrington and Bebbington (1993) emphasize, NGOs are very context dependent. They operate in a variety of local, regional, and national political environments which may or may not support the formation of democratic organizations. For example, the public and private sectors may see such collective-democratic NGOs as a challenge to the *status quo* bureaucratic and centralized organizational environments.

Second, NGOs have social histories (Farrington and Bebbington, 1993). Many have evolved out of their Founders' concerns and actions, such that at present their structure is firmly established. The original organizational form was more a means to the end of changing societal conditions, rather than a goal in itself. That is, the organizational structure was not necessarily predesigned before its workers began practising. Thus, can an existing NGO radically change its present structure in order to mirror its democratic societal functions?

Another question to consider is how much the concept of organizational democracy explains project effectiveness in the field. A key claim made about NGOs is that they are flexible and responsive to the local situation and their clients. This suggests that the effectiveness of the NGO, say a GSO, and the projects it supports depends largely on the quality of its workers' verbal communication skills. That is, that there are full and open discussions between workers and clients regarding local problems, possible solutions and project progress. I would suggest, on the basis of the proposition from participatory democratic theory and collectives' experiences that decision making participation has an educative effect on participants, that those NGOs that were structured democratically would be those in which authority is delegated, and open to recall particularly between all types of NGO workers. If this was the case inside the NGO, then I suspect that the NGO's workers would transfer their experience of authority delegation and recall to their relationship with their members, during the process of carrying out projects. Accountability between workers in the NGO could translate into accountability between workers and their members.

In summary, while organizational empowerment may be desirable to some types of NGOs, its feasibility depends on certain conditions and is subject to certain constraints.

The above discussion has attempted to highlight and analyse the prescriptive claim made by NGO analysts that NGOs, in general, should operate democratically, and thus deal with the question of to whom they are accountable. Interestingly, some NGOs, of different types, are themselves expressing a desire to match their societal democratic ideals with their own organizational operation. Exploring the theory of participatory or direct democracy, and experience of workplace democracy as a form of organizational democracy, helped to define what an extreme form of organizational 'self-management' means. Applying this concept and practice to NGOs in general creates problems as NGOs are diverse. Thus it is suggested that different forms of democracy potentially could operate in different types of NGOs. Overall, a political analysis of NGOs is shown to uncover a detailed understanding of how NGOs operate as organizations, specifically as they parallel different systems of government.

References

Bernstein, P. (1982), 'Necessary Elements for Effective Worker Participation in Decision-Making' in Lindenfeld, F. and Rothschild-Whitt, J. (eds), *Workplace Democracy and Social Change*, Porter Sargent Publishers, Boston.

Billis, D. (1989), 'A Theory of the Voluntary Sector: Implications for Policy and Practice', *Working Paper 5*, Centre for Voluntary Organization, LSE, London.

Billis, D. and Mackeith, J. (1992), 'Growth and Change in NGOs: Concepts and Comparative experience' in Edwards, M. and Hulme, D. (eds), *Making a Difference: NGOs and Development in a Changing World*, Earthscan Publications Ltd., London.

Bratton, M. (1989), 'The politics of government-NGO relations in Africa' in *World Development*, vol. 17, no. 4.

Brown, L.D. and Covey, J.G. (1989), 'Organization Development in Social Change Organizations: Some Implications for Practice' in Sikes, W., Drexler, A., Grant, J. (eds), *The Emerging Practice of Organization Development*, NTL Institute for Applied Behavioral Science and California University Association Inc., Virginia.

Clark, J. (1991), *Democratizing Development: The Role of Voluntary Organizations*, Earthscan Publications Ltd., London.

Dennison, G. (1972), *The Lives of Children: The Story of the First Street School*, Penguin Books, Middlesex.

Edwards, M. and Hulme, D. (1994), 'NGOs and Development: Performance and Accountability in the "New World Order"', Background Paper for Conference at University of Manchester, 27-29 June 1994, Manchester.

Edwards, M. and Hulme, D. (1992), 'Scaling-up the Developmental Impact of NGOs: Concepts and Experiences' in Edwards, M. and Hulme, D. (eds), *Making a Difference: NGOs and Development in a Changing World*, Earthscan Publications Ltd., London.

Esman, M.J. and Uphoff, N.T. (1984), *Local Organizations: Intermediaries in Rural Development*, Cornell University Press, Ithaca.

Farrington, J. and Bebbington, A. (1993), *Reluctant Partners? Non-Governmental Organisations, The State and Sustainable Agricultural Development*, Routledge, London.

Fowler, A. (1988), 'NGOs in Africa: Achieving Comparative Advantage in Relief and Micro-Development', *IDS Discussion Paper* No. 29, Institute of Development Studies, Sussex, August.

Hannan, A. (1995), 'NGOs as Development Agencies in Bangladesh: A Critical Overview', Paper presented at In-House Workshop on NGOs, School of Development Studies, University of East Anglia, 15-17 January 1995, Norwich.

Hodson, R. (1992), 'Small, Medium or Large: The Rocky Road to NGO Growth' in Edwards, M. and Hulme, D. (eds), *Making a Difference: NGOs and Development in a Changing World*, Earthscan Publications Ltd., London.

Korten, D. (1987), 'Third generation NGO strategies: a key to people-centred development' in *World Development*, vol. 15, Supplement.

Lindenfeld, F. and Rothschild-Whitt, J. (eds) (1982), *Workplace Democracy and Social Change*, Porter Sargent Publishers, Boston.

Morgan, G. (1986), *Images of Organization*, Sage Publications, London.

Pateman, C. (1970), *Participation and Democratic Theory*, Cambridge University Press.

PRIA (1991), *Voluntary Development Organisations in India: A Study of History, Roles and Future Challenges*, Society for Participatory Research in Asia (PRIA), New Delhi.

PRIA (1988), *Report of International Forum on Participatory Evaluation*, 1-5 March, PRIA, New Delhi.

Robinson, M. (1991), 'Evaluating the Impact of NGOs in Rural Poverty Alleviation: India Country Study', *Working Paper* no. 49, Overseas Development Institute, London.

Rondinelli, D.A. (1990), *Development Projects as Policy Experiments: An Adaptive Approach to Development Administration*, Routledge, London.

Rothschild, J. and Whitt, J.A. (1986), *The Cooperative Workplace: Potentials and Dilemmas of Organizational Democracy and Participation*, Cambridge University Press, Cambridge.

For Product Safety Concerns and Information please contact our EU
representative GPSR@taylorandfrancis.com Taylor & Francis Verlag GmbH,
Kaufingerstraße 24, 80331 München, Germany

Printed and bound by CPI Group (UK) Ltd, Croydon, CR0 4YY
08/05/2025
01864382-0003